COLLECTED POEMS

Mary Symon

for

STANLEY WALSINGHAM
(1961-2019)

COLLECTED
POEMS

Mary Symon

with a preface and introduction by
Ian Spring & Fred Freeman

Second impression 2020
by Rymour Books
with Hog's Back Press
45 Needless Road
PERTH
PH2 0LE

© the editors 2020
ISBN 978-0-9540704-5-8

Cover design by Ian Spring
Typeset in Bembo
Printed and bound by
Imprint Digital
Seychelles Farm
Upton Pyne
Exeter

Supported by The Scottish Poetry Library and the Doric Board

Scottish **Poetry** Library
Bringing people and poems together

THE
DORIC
BOARD

The paper used in this book is approved
by the Forest Stewardship Council

FSC

CONTENTS

MEDITATIONS

ACKNOWLEDGEMENTS

The editors are grateful to Edinburgh University Library, the National Library of Scotland, the Michell Library, Glasgow, the Imperial War Museum and Robert Gordon's College, Aberdeen for access to their collections.

We are grateful to Gordon Hay for reading and commenting on the text. Stanley Walsingham did some of the research for this book but, regretfully, did not live to see its completion.

PREFACE

It is fair to say that not only have the great literary figures of the twentieth century cast a long shadow over more minor poets like Mary Symon (or Violet Jacob and others, for that matter), but Symon's place in the Scots tradition has never been properly recognised. It has been obfuscated by diehard views of what constitutes real literature in Scotland; the very same views that prevent due recognition of the remarkable achievement of the Scottish folk movement despite the international praise of, for example, E P Thompson, Bob Dylan or Nelson Mandela.

It is a blinkered vision of culture which, were it applied to, say, European fine art, would lead us to the untenable conclusion that a more vernacular artist like Bruegel or Daumier is not to be considered alongside Raphael or David. What utter nonsense. And, thankfully, not the case.

Yes, in recent years, there has been more official support for vernacular traditions amongst our educators and arts awarding bodies; but, there still persists a very elitist, constipated notion regarding Scots language and its place in our culture. If this were not the case, Mary Symon's *Deveron Days*, her collection of poems, would not have remained out of print from 1938 to the present day, and poets of the stature of Lewis Spence would not continue to be out of print—the most recent edition of his *Collected Poems* dating from 1953. Little has moved on from Hugh MacDiarmid's snide, demeaning remarks about Mary Symon: namely, citing her simian ignorance of 'the processes of evolution [that] have carried the Scottish nation far beyond the hill-plaid and 'sleevid weskit' stage'; and her perverse adherence to the benighted tradition of what he refers to as 'Doric infantilism':

For the most part the Doric tradition serves to condone mental inertia cloaking mental paucity with a trivial and ridiculously over-valued pawkiness! And it bolsters up that instinctive suspicion of cleverness and culture—so strongly in all peasants... Scotland stagnates in an apparently permanent literary infancy owing to the operation of certain forces of which the Doric sentiment is the principal.[1]

If we juxtapose these remarks with his other damning observations regarding folk culture, published forty years later in the *Scotsman*, we begin to understand more fully the elitist nature of the social and cultural divides (for the two go hand-in-hand) which continue to make it so very difficult to measure the true worth of the Scots tradition in literature and song, and to convince our educators and our children to take serious interest in it:

> The demand everywhere today is for higher and higher intellectual levels. Why should we be concerned then with songs which reflect the educational limitations, the narrow lives, the poor literary abilities, of a peasantry we have happily outgrown? The study of such productions may be of some historical value, but is certainly of no literary value... surely our regard and, if possible, emulation, should be given to the best and not to the lowest in past literary productivity.[2]

And herein resides the crux of the matter: the arbitrary (and damaging) notion of a social and historical wedge in Scottish culture whereby art is by definition the preserve of one very select, elitist group: a group whom Burns once sarcastically described as 'the jury'.[3] Avowedly, this is part of a national myth which took root in Scottish Enlightenment thinking as the literati cast a jaundiced eye over the 'dark ages' of a very fragmented history: from the Reformation through the seventeenth century (never mind the considerable achievements of The Advocates' Library (now the National Library of Scotland); the Botanic Garden; the widely celebrated Edinburgh Medical School of the late seventeenth century). Moreover, this was a conscious historical trade-off, so sharply delineated in David Hume's buoyant letter to Gilbert Elliot, where he describes what it means for Scotland to be a success in Britain and modern Europe in social, cultural and political terms. And it is particularly noteworthy that the 'very corrupt Dialect', to which he refers, is an integral part of that trade-off. It patently has no place within the 'distinguish'd Literature' for which he so wantonly enthuses:

Is it not strange that, at a time when we have lost our Princes, our Parliaments, our independent Government, even the Presence of our chief Nobility, are unhappy, in our Accent & Pronunciation, speak a corrupt Dialect of the Tongue which we make use of; is it not strange, I say, that, in these Circumstances, we shou'd really be the People most distinguish'd for Literature in Europe?[4]

Little wonder that others of his contemporaries, like Lord Kames, for example, saw progress somewhat differently: as a 'Janus double-fac'd' mixed blessing and curse.[5] Hume was, unquestionably one of our greatest historical figures, but, along with many other Enlightenment thinkers, he left Scotland with a destructive cultural legacy: a national myth in which Scots language is seen as inherently 'corrupt', insular, reactionary. A myth not even tempered by a balanced philosophical reflection on his own historical position and of the obvious power play at work in the mid eighteenth century. He fails, or refuses, to see that. It would take a much lesser figure from a later period, Max Weinreich, to appreciate the unenviable position of minority cultures and languages. As he claims in his pithy defence of Yiddish: 'A shprakh iz a dialekt mit an armey un flot' (A language is a dialect with an army and a navy. [6]

But that is not a point that has been fully digested even yet. It is, in fact, easy to mark a straight line from Hume's historically based assertions to those of Edwin Muir, damning vernacular Scots language and literature for evermore. Here is Muir in full flight on the subject:

…it is clear that the Reformation, the Union of the Crowns, and the Union of the Kingdoms had all a great deal to do with it (the disintegration of the language of Scottish literature)… I must confine myself… to certain of its consequences. The prerequisite of an autonomous literature is a homogeneous language. If Shakespeare had written in the dialect of Warwickshire, Spenser in Cockney, Raleigh in the broad Western speech which he used, the future of English literature must have been very different, for it would have lacked a common language where all the thoughts and feelings of the English people could come together; add a lustre to one another; and serve as a standard for one another... without it no people can have any standard of literature. For this homogeneous language is the only means yet discovered for expressing the response of a whole people, emotional and intellectual... And since some time in the sixteenth century Scotland has lacked such a language... Scottish poetry exists in a vacuum: it neither acts on the rest of literature nor reacts to it: and consequently it has shrunk to the level of anonymous folk-song... Scots has survived to our time as a language for simple poetry and the simpler kind of short story... it expresses therefore only a fragment of the Scottish mind... For, reduced to its simplest terms, this linguistic division means that Scotsmen feel in one language and think in another...[7]

Thus, we have a mythos, based upon false premises, that has, for so long, done our critical thinking for us. And it is embodied in simple, facile shibboleths like 'wholeness'; 'fragment'; 'division'; 'homogeneous language'.

It was natural, then, for Hugh MacDiarmid and his coterie to advocate the creation of an experimental, 'synthetic' Scots based, somewhat, upon Middle Scots. So, he would urge the literateurs: 'Not Burns —Dunbar': urge, quite generally, a return to the 'human wholeness' of the Scottish medieval tradition over the couthie, insular tradition of the Vernacular Revival. As Muir has it: 'If Henryson and Dunbar had written prose they would have written in the same language as they used for poetry, for their minds were still whole'.[8]

And the modern literati would arm themselves with so many carefully garnered, but specious, examples in support of their point. For example, in his influential *Scott and Scotland*, Muir compares two lyrics on love to prove that the medieval poet maturely 'thinks and feels with equal intensity, on the same plane and in the same language' whilst the vernacular poet expresses 'a mere effusion of thoughtless emotion'.[9]

Luve is ane fervent fire,
Kendillit without desire;
  Short plesour, lang displesour,
Repentance is the hire;
  Ane puir tressour without mesour:
Luve is ane fervent fire.

(Alexander Scott)

But a' the pleasures e'er I saw,
  Tho' three times doubl'd fairly,
That happy night was worth them a',
  Amang the rigs o' barley.

(Robert Burns)

How unfair. He compares apples and oranges: one, being a serious philosophical poem on the nature of formal love; the other, a
bit of light-hearted banter and self-satire on male bravado. Moreover, the eighteenth-century printer has corrupted the text with all his
apostrophes and lapses into standard English ('pleasures... doubl'd...
night...'). We might as well make invidious comparisons between
Claude Lorrain's 'Landscape with Dancing Figures' and Bruegel's 'The
Fight between Carnival and Lent'. Are both not landscape paintings?
Indeed, they are. But, one is a more formalised work with its philosophical credentials all to the fore; the other, a lively representation
of contemporary humanity caught in the act, holding-up, as Hogarth
would have it, a mirror to humanity; directing us, in its own lighter,
comic way to serious reflection over the course of time. It is all in the
way the comic, the grotesque in art can, so subtlety, present us with
more than meets the eye at first glance: so often, presenting us with
two texts: one for immediate consumption; the other for more considered thought.

To return to Burns, and to be fair to him, let us consider a love song
with a bit more gravitas about it than his *Corn Rigs*. Take *John Anderson,*

My Jo: a prime example of a seemingly couthie vernacular song which, so intimately, makes a moving, universal statement about the human condition. More to the point, it achieves this through a powerfully hybridised (sophisticated) use of language: colloquial Scots idioms and forms; the high register of Scots language; straight neoclassical English and more—all labouring to express the compassion of an old wifie for her failing husband.

John Anderson my jo, John,
Whan we were first acquent,
Your locks were like the raven,
Your bonie brow was brent;
But now your brow is beld, John,
Your locks are like the snaw,
But blessins on your frosty pow,
  John Anderson, my jo!

If this is supposed to represent a fragmented, bastardised use of language, the utterance of a less than 'whole' artist and human being, it does so with words and idioms that would not have been unfamiliar to the Medieval Makars: words like 'acquent', from Old French; 'brent', from ancient Anglian; English lines like 'Yer locks were like the raven'. Even with the printer's corruption of the text—'now' for 'noo', etc—the strength of the passage remains.

Moreover, so many of the linguistic hallmarks of the medieval tradition are here in evidence: interlocked alliteration patterns (eg, those 'b's') to suggest the emotional breathlessness of the old wife—'bonie... brow... brent... brow... beld... blessins'; anaphora—'Your locks were... Your locks are', 'But noo... But blessins', the constantly ringing repetition 'John... John... John... John'—for the intimacy of address; the use of monosyllables throughout for reflective emphasis on each word—'But... noo... yer... brow... is... beld'. Furthermore, there is more than a hint of the direct address, monologue and dialogue, of the ballads here which Edwin Muir, for one, valued as great literature: ballads like *Skippin Barfit* or

My Son David. In short, this is a finely distilled expression of serious, thoughtful human emotion; not an example of corrupted language or low art.

This brief analysis of *John Anderson, My Jo* thus begs all sorts of questions. And foremost amongst them: to what extent does the Vernacular Scots tradition actually manifest attributes of the art of the Makars, or of the traditional ballads? Since the primary objections of the modern period centre round vernacular language itself and the fragmented nature of the Scots vernacular tradition for the expression of human emotion, it is sobering to note that a ballad scholar such as Hamish Henderson regards ballad-Scots and its relation to folk art as having linguistic strengths rather than weaknesses:

> [Ballad-Scots is] a flexible formulaic language which grazes ballad-English and yet is clearly identifiable as a distinct folk-literary lingo... [It admirably manifests] a curious 'bilingualism' in one language which greatly extends its range and demonstrably makes it a much suppler instrument than the rather wooden 'ballad-English'... In the folk field, as well as in the less sure-footed literary Lallans, Scots may be said to 'include English and go beyond it'.[10]

This is, of course, a counter-argument to MacDiarmid and Muir, and constitutes something of a lone voice on the subject. As such, it bears closer scrutiny; throws us back on ourselves; back to a re-evaluation of our history and tradition overall.

Implicit in Henderson's bold assertion is an argument that would not have been alien to, say, Issac Bashevis Singer in his championing Yiddish for serious literature. And, in certain respects—but not in all, the Vernacular Scots—English language debate is just a re-run of the Hebrew vs Yiddish flyting. Might not the unhomogeneous Scots language tradition of flux and fragmentation be more representative of the universal human condition as Singer found Yiddish was for the fragmented experience of the archetypal 'wandering Jew'; or, more generally, for the experience of minority cultures wherever they be? As Singer so beautifully puts it:

The Yiddish-speaking Jew, his fear of physical and spiritual efface-
ment, his desperate effort to sustain the values and languages of his
history, his struggle for independence and his actual dependence on
the good will of others—this Jew symbolizes to me the whole human species. Man must be both himself and an integrated part of
the whole, loyal to his own home and origin and deeply cognizant
of the origin of others.[11]

Furthermore, and on a different tack, Scotland has always been a
cultural and linguistic hybrid with its Celts of all kin-kind (Picts, Bry-
thonic tribes, Scotti); its Angles, Vikings, Flemings and French. And,
with its proximity to England, the much larger nation, and with its
European Latinate roots, close analysis reveals that Middle Scots literature was itself a linguistic amalgam which reflected its geographical
and cultural position: high and low registers of Scots; aureate Latin,
Old French and more. But this is a subject beyond the sphere of this
appreciation.

What can safely be argued is that, in general terms, duality is more
fundamental to the Scottish psyche (and art) than some unattainable
Platonic ideal of wholeness or homogeneity. And it has absolutely
no bearing on emotional immaturity, linguistically or otherwise. Geographically, we live across cultures and languages: England—Scotland;
Highlands—Lowlands; Lowlands—Borders; Hebridean Isles—Norse
Isles; and linguistically, Scots—Gaelic; English—Scots; Gaelic—English; and so many variants of both Scots (like the Doric and Central
Scots) and Gaelic. Manifest as well, and we see this in the very archi-
tecture of our cities all round us, is a strong contrast between more or-
ganically formed old towns and more classically conceived new towns.
It is a clash of opposites: a tug-o-war between what Sydney Goodsir
Smith identifies as a Gothic-Celtic asymmetry and a Classical symme-
try.[12] Moreover, the city, as Lewis Mumford notes in *The City in History*,
transmits 'in symbolic forms and human patterns a representative por-
tion of a culture'.[13] In Scotland it is a palpable symbol of a culture with
interesting dualities and tensions that embodies our social and historical position in the world. And, it can be argued that, like our architec-

ture, our vernacular Scots literature embraces these self-same dualities and tensions. As such, it is a just representation of who we are; not a falsification of who we might be when we look over our shoulders.

To argue more directly: Muir, MacDiarmid and the others have grasped the thin end of the wedge. For one can trace this theme of duality right throughout the Scots tradition in literature: from ballads as mundane as *Sir Patrick Spens* and *The Twa Corbies* through the verse of the Medieval Makars and the Vernacular Revivalists (Fergusson, Burns and the others); the poetry and song of our twentieth century literature—right across the board. This is the glue that, in fact, does, perhaps ironically, bind the Scots tradition together. Consider, for example, a few lines from Dunbar's philosophical poem on the duality of existence: *Of the Changes of Life*, where he ponders the human condition ('this warld unstabille') and his own futile search for stability ('Concluding all in my contrair'). And Dunbar will use a significant metaphor here to express that duality; a metaphor so rooted in Scottish art that it pervades the tradition of poetry and song; a metaphor that would be as familiar to Mary Symon as it would have been to Robert Fergusson or Robert Burns. It is a pastoral / counter-pastoral metaphor that, notably, embraces the duality under discussion. Take, for example, the last two stanzas of Dunbar's poem:

Yisterday fair up sprang the flouris:
This day thai ar all slane with schouris
And fowlis in forrest that sang cleir
Now walkis with a drery cheir
Full cauld ar baith their beddis and bouris

So nixt to symmer wyntir bene
Nixt dirk mednycht the mirthefull morrow
Nixt efter confort cairis kene
Nixt efter jye aye cummis sorrow
So is this warld and ay hes bene

Mutability; the unremitting passage of time; the uncertainty of human existence: it is all expressed so intensely, so vividly through this pastoral / counter-pastoral duality and tension. To cite the most obvious examples:

> Yisterday fair… flouris (PASTORAL)
> This day… schouris (COUNTER-PASTORAL)
> symmer… winter (PASTORAL / COUNTER-PASTORAL)
> confort… cairis kene (PASTORAL / COUNTER-PASTORAL)
> jye… sorrow (PASTORAL / COUNTER-PASTORAL)

Moreover, Dunbar does not draw upon a 'homogeneous' language. It is, rather, a thoroughgoing hybrid with many English words and spellings in evidence; a colourful interweaving of high and low registers of Scots; Latinate words like 'convenabille', 'dessaveabille'. More to the point, when Dunbar needs to make a more sympathetic statement (as with his brief reflection on the birds 'Full cauld'), or a more personal statement, as it were a final riposte, he does not revert to English or even Latin, both of which are, for him, too distant and abstract. He reverts to the everyday tongue of the common Scots man and woman; for it is the only personal voice he can honestly draw upon in presenting the reader with an intimate perspective of his own thoughts and feelings. It is precisely what every great poet from Wordsworth to Yeats and T S Eliot was driving at with all the agonising over simple poetic voice and direct expression. It is, in fact, the vernacular Scots we still speak in the present day—as common as the Border's saying: 'It's aye been': 'So is this warld and ay hes bene'.

It is also the voice Mary Symon will draw upon in her poetry along with all the other finely honed techniques of Dunbar and the Makars: the pastoral / counter-pastoral duality; the superabundance of interlocked alliteration patterns; the rhetorical use of anaphora for emphasis; registers of language for effect.

And, it is an awareness, no less than that of a Singer or a Chaim Potok—yes, of alienation, fragmentation, disunity, but; at the same time, of an endeavour, each time the turmoil erupts in our history, to regroup and forge a new synthesis. It is the universal human struggle, so directly and simply expressed in, for example, Burns's uprooted moose in the field with the forlorn subsistence farmer by his side earnestly contemplating the duality of his existence in poignant Scots vernacular lines like these:

But Och! I backward cast my ee,
  On prospects drear!
An forward, tho I canna see,
  I guess an fear!

A 'mere effusion of thoughtless emotion'? Or such memorable lines that they would suggest an apt allusion for John Steinbeck in *Of Mice And Men*? Could these lines have been better expressed, more emotionally stated, through a more formal, higher utterance in English? Or is there a clarity, a directness of statement inherent in both the vernacular Scots of the period and in the poetic voice here speaking it? It is all a matter of proximity, perspective. It is, for example, the communal voice of Hamish Henderson, himself a soldier in the field, summarising in one meaningful line (in his *Banks of Sicily*) the feelings and sentiments of his overly exhausted troops: 'Puir bliddy swaddies are wearie'. These are his (and his men's) most personal thoughts; for they are utterly spent, and there is more blood on the horizon.

Not the typical, monumental words of the war poets—no; but the bare, emotive words of a Scots sodger and poet in the field, pretty well at his wit's end. Not a dilution of emotion, or a suspension of serious thought and reflection.

So what elevates a poem like Mary Symon's *The Soldiers' Cairn*, with its somewhat remote rural North-east setting.? What makes it the powerful literary statement that it is, well beyond the confines of kailyard literature or 'Doric infantilism'?

As mentioned earlier, the Scots vernacular tradition often reflowers at times of major upheaval—periods of alienation, fragmentation, disunity. The major upheaval in this case? The First World War, and the all pervasive sense of loss as a small community endeavours to cope with inexplicable and irrational devastation; as it endeavours to bury its dead; regroup, redefine itself as a cohesive community and, then, emotionally, move on.

Wherein resides the high seriousness that MacDiarmid and Muir insisted was so conspicuously missing from a poem like this one? We have argued that, in fact, the great severance between the medieval tradition and that of the Scots vernacular revival is something of a chimera. Yes, the traditions evolved in two wholly different political entities: one an independent Scotland with its own king and court; the other, a somewhat diminished country in terms of its political power and self-esteem. And the mix of registers of Scots used reflects this cultural change. Moreover, the periods differ stylistically and rhetorically. Would it make sense to compare the English of John Donne with that of Bob Dylan? Nonetheless, as Hamish Henderson has noted, the two traditions in Scotland have never been mutually exclusive:

> Throughout Scottish history there has been a constant interplay between the folk tradition and the learned literary tradition—an interplay more constant and fruitful with us than in the literatures of most other European countries.[14]

We see much of that constant interplay in the use of the pastoral metaphor over the centuries: from ballads like *Skippin Barfit* to Dunbar's most serious philosophical poems and, here, Mary Symon's *The Soldiers' Cairn*.[15] And it is this pastoral/ counter-pastoral tension that provides a tightly knit artistic structure to the work. Like Dunbar's *Of the Changes of Life*, the poem sets into bold relief the poignancy of its message with its simple pastoral contrasts. For example:

(PASTORAL = LIFE, SERENITY & BEAUTY—first verse)

Gie me a hill wi the heather on't,
  An a reid sun drappin doon,
Or the mists o the mornin risin saft
  Wi the reek owre a wee grey toon.
Gie me a howe by the lang Glen road,

For it's there mang the whin an fern…

(COUNTER-PASTORAL = DEATH & SADNESS—second verse)

Far awa is the Flanders land
  Wi fremmit France atween,
But mony a howe o them baith the day
  Has a hap o the Gordon green.
It's them we kent that's lyin there,
  An it's nae wi stane or airn
But wi brakin herts, an mem'ries sair,
  That we're biggin the Sodgers' Cairn.

(PASTORAL = PAST LIFE—third verse)

  Doon, laich doon the Dullan sings—
    An I ken o an aul sauch tree,
  Where a wee loon's wahnie's hingin yet…

(COUNTER-PASTORAL = DEATH / MUTABILITY)

  …That's deid in Picardy;
An ilka win fae the Conval's broo
  Bends aye the buss o ern,
Where aince he futtled a name that noo
  I'll read on the Sodgers' Cairn.

Moreover, vivid imagery underpins the notion of a pastoral past as against a counter-pastoral present. The natural rich growth of the hills —the 'whin an fern' of the idyllic opening verse has, for example, been supplanted by a poignant image of anti-nature: the harrowing growth in foreign lands of corpses: the 'Gordon green', rather than the green of the plants, that now covers the hills.

> But mony a howe o them baith the day
> Has a hap o the Gordon green.

The idyllic memories of the 'Dullan' and the 'aul sauch tree', where the wahnie's 'hingin yet' are, again, only painful reminders of all thought that has been stripped down to a simple contrasting duality between past life and present death—the loon 'That's deid in Picardy'. And it is a pattern of trenchant imagery, representing an entire community's divided thought, that is so exquisitely sustained through the language and linguistic technique running throughout the poem: the poignantly antithetical images of, for example, hard 'stane or airn' and 'brakin herts'. It is the Makars' art of tragic detail and simple juxtaposition: like Dunbar's 'symmer... winter' / 'jye... sorrow'.

Closely aligned with that imagery is a masterful control of pacing married to a Makar's deployment of all the high artistic techniques we have come to associate with the medieval tradition: interlocked alliteration patterns and internal rhyme to slow the pace; the principle of sound = sense united with syllabic variation (monosyllables, disyllables) in underpinning pastoral contrasts; rhetorical repetition for emphasis and effect; the subtle use of mixed voice and language, Scots and English.

There is, overall, a tightly knit structure (a unity of effect) widely built round alliteration, internal rhyme and rhetorical repetition patterns. And this serves to create a sombre mood and tempo to the scene, whereby the physical pacing of the community up the hill is felt empathetically by the reader. In this connection, every verse begins with an interlocked alliteration pattern, to slow the pace, underline the sobriety of the occasion, and ends with a rhetorical repetition on the central focus: 'the Sodgers' cairn'. Just consider the gentler, alliterative patterns of the first verse which set the scene of lost pastoral: all the h's ('hill... heather'), d's ('drappin doon'), atmospheric sibilant s's so suggestive of the gentle breeze and sway of the 'whin' and 'fern' ('sun... mists... risin... saft'); the elongated vowel sounds—and internal rhymes, always present in pastoral verse and song—like the long e, double ee, ie and short i sounds: 'Gie... me... wi... reid... reek...

wee... me... ye'; the rhythm of the disyllables creating a very mixed pastoral flow—like heartbeats ('hea-ther... drap-pin... mor-nin... ris-in... hear-in'). Or the rhythm of the faltering anapaests hemmed-in by monosyllables (like the rising and falling of a person breathing with sighs; not at all the unremitting anapaests of the drum-roll beats of, say, Sir Patrick Spens's men riding frantically to their ship).

> Or the mists... o the morn-in risin saft
> Wi the reek... owre a wee... grey toon

It is all so obviously cast in the whole idiom of elegiac verse: like, for example, Gray's *Elegy Written in a Country Churchyard*. What can Muir be thinking when he maintains: 'Scottish poetry exists in a vacuum: it neither acts on the rest of literature nor reacts to it'? This is not to argue that, with *The Soldiers' Cairn*, Symon alludes to Gray; but, only to observe that she undoubtedly writes with a strong sense of the literary tradition of Scots and English elegiac verse behind her. Just consider the slow pacing of Gray's opening verse with its alliterative p's and w's to the fore: ('parting... plowman... plods... weary... way... world'); its disyllables like heartbeats ('cur-few... part-ing... low-ing... slow-ly...', etc); its internal rhymes ('lowing... slowly'); its rhetorical repetitions ('The cur-few... The low-ing... The plow-man'). The point is not that Gray writes about a very rural scene in anything like the same idiom as Mary Symon, for Gray's verse is far more overtly philosophical; formalised.

But both poets do employ techniques of language, particularly of pacing, that characterise the Scots and English tradition of elegiac verse, and underpin its high seriousness. For example, in Gray's use of, firstly, alliteration, and, secondly, anapaests:

> The curfew tolls the knell of parting day,
> The lowing herd wind slowly o'er the lea,
> The plowman homeward plods his weary way
> And leaves the world to darkness and to me...
> Oft... did the har-vest... to their sickle... yield...

Similarly, in the second verse of *The Soldiers' Cairn*, there is, again, an interlocked alliteration pattern; this time more impassioned, counter-pastoral in character with its f's, so often used in Middle Scots literature to suggest the flapping of birds' wings in desperate flight, as in Henryson's *Preichin o the Swallow* ('far... Flanders... fremmit... France); its h's ('howe... Has... hap'); its harder sounding b's, mainly monosyllables, suggesting the heavy breathing—a 'buh... buh... buh' effect and more emphatic expression ('But... baith... But... brakin'). Here, in dwelling on the grief of death in battle, sound = sense. More end-stop, biting, mainly monosyllabic words are used to conjure-up painful cutting feelings: hard end-stop t's ('fremmit... atween... but... it's... kent... that's... But... herts... That'). And those disyllabic words, so suggestive of heartbeats, are here again to the fore: 'a-wa... Flanders... frem-mit... at-ween... mon-y... Gor-don... ly-in... brak-in... mem'-ries'.

In part, the third verse reverts back to pastoral: a whimsical reflection on a happy childhood in the not so distant past. Thus it starts with softer interlocked alliteration patterns: d's ('Doon... doon... Dullan') and sibilant s's, ch's and ce's, once again conjuring-up a gentle breeze and the mollifying song of the river—'the Dullan sings' ('laich... sings... sauch... loon's... wahnie's... buss... aince'). And, in the main, long vowel sounds shore-up the soft pastoral rhetoric: long oo's, ee's, ie's, short i's ('Doon... doon... sings... tree... wee... wahnie's... hingin'). The exception to the whole mellifluous pastoral flow is an abrupt interruption, set-off with four bluntly and emphatically highlighted words: three monosyllables that stop the flow and, then, setting the line into stark relief, the only trisyllable in the entire poem ('That's deid in... Pi-car-dy').

The fourth verse opens with a hard interlocked alliteration pattern of b's and t's coupled with a strong rhetorical repetition ('build it... build it... Till... to') importuning the community, with steely determination, in a more formal register of language; not at all the patois of everyday colloquial speech: that familiar language of warm communal interaction that we hear in that conversational voice of the opening verse with its Scots idioms and grammatical construction: 'D'ye mind on't, Will? Are ye hearin, Dod'?

It is, rather, by contrast, a much colder, distant language: yes, the English of officialdom; yes, the English of the pulpit; yes the English that will, in fact, be engraved on the stone monument. But it is not deployed here because only 'a fragment of the Scottish mind' can ever be expressed in the Doric, or because 'Scottish poetry exists in a vacuum' and, must, perforce, resort to English language for serious utterance.

There are times when language needs to be unfamiliar (wholly removed from human commerce and conversation); set into relief like a timeless engraving. As the poet, Michael Hamburger, reminds us: '... in order to be rich the word in poetry 'must first become strange'.'[16] The language here, like the stone monument, is itself quite remote from this rural community: not something animate and of this world. It is a more symbolic expression far removed from the animated life of the community—'more than death is symbolled there, Than tears or triumphs by'—something that strangely heals in its timelessness, coldness, remoteness from the community. It is exactly what Chris Guthrie is driving at in her pondering at the Standing Stones of Kinraddie when she finds it 'strange and comforting... the only place where ever she could come and stand back a little from the clamour of the days'.[17]

By contrast, the fifth verse returns to the moment at hand and the familiar Doric of the community; but, with its interlocked, alliterative liquid 'l' sounds, suggests something very close to the folk, right at that moment, as they climb the 'hameland hill'. It is very like the haunting music of the church bells with its plangent ell... ell... ell... refrain: ('Lads... lyin... lands... you'll... lanely... hill... love... we'll... cradle's... that'll'). The simplicity and directness of the sentiments mask the intricacy of Symon's poetic technique.

And, however one wishes to interpret that last verse, the duality of human experience is ever present. Mary Symon will state it so very simply in those closing lines which advert to the life cycle of the sodgers—from birth to death, and the abiding memories of new life that they leave behind. For they were once bairns (she addresses them—'Oh, my Bairn, my Bairn') and, as such, possess a healing, rejuvenating power even in death. Structurally, the poem has moved, tightly, from life to death: from the picturesque, ideally conceived 'hill' setting of the living, social 'toon' (the 'hill wi' heather o't') to the 'hameland hill' with its 'lanely cairn'.

But, there is here a note of measured emotional acceptance, if not of optimism—neither wholly pastoral nor counter-pastoral: 'love' being the only thing that endures beyond the duality of these catastrophic human circumstances.

Hardly 'a mere effusion of thoughtless emotion'. At the end, the bittersweet pastoral music of 'a cradle's croon': those carefully crafted and spaced long vowels and internal rhymes of hers: 'braw-aa… croon-doon… Tae-fae'.

But oh, my Bairn, my Bairn
It's a cradle's croon that'll aye blaw doon
Tae me fae the Sodgers' Cairn.

We are again reminded of duality: Grassic Gibbon's poignant words: 'Life is an unending fight—between evil and good, darkness and light, death and life.'[18]

And we are reminded as well that it is by dint of 'love' alone that the Sodgers' Cairn, so like the soldiers' monument at the end of *Sunset Song*,[19] speaks for the 'enduring love' of a community.

This lanely cairn on a hameland hill
Is aa that oor love can dee…

Fred Freeman

NOTES

1. Letter to *Aberdeen Free Press,* 30th January 1922, in Alan Bold (ed.), *The Letters of Hugh MacDiarmid* (Hamish Hamilton: London, 1984), p. 754.

2. Hugh MacDiarmid to the Scotsman—7th March 1964, Alec Finlay (ed.) *The Armstrong Nose: Selected Letters of Hamish Henderson,* (Polygon: Edinburgh, 1996), p. 119.

3. Letter to Reverend John Skinner, Edinburgh 25th October 1787, James A MacKay (ed.), *The Complete Letters of Robert Burns,* (Alloway Publishing: Alloway, 1987) p. 363.

4. Letter to Gilbert Elliot of Minto, 1757, J Y T Greig (ed.), *The Letters of David Hume,* (Oxford University Press: Oxford, 1969), Vol 1, p. 255.

5. Kames refers specifically to greed and the obsession with property, but his arguments reveal a disenchantment with progress overall. Henry Home, Lord Kames, *Sketches On The History Of Man,* (W Strahan & T Cadell: Edinburgh 1774) Vol. 1, p. 67.

6. A statement by Weinreich at a YIVO conference, 5th January, 1945.

7. Edwin Muir, *Scott and Scotland* (Polygon: Edinburgh 1982) (edited by Alan Massie), pp 7-8.

8. Edwin Muir, *Scott and Scotland* (Polygon: Edinburgh 1982) (edited by Alan Massie), p. 8.

9. Edwin Muir, *Scott and Scotland* (Polygon: Edinburgh 1982) (edited by Alan Massie), p. 12.

10. Hamish Henderson, 'The Ballads', in *Alias MacAlias* (Polygon: Edinburgh, 1992), pp 23-27, p. 27. In fact, Henderson wrote to Muir and insisted: 'I'm inclined to think that the folk poetry of Scotland is superior to most 'art' poetry. I am sure now that nothing should be said about the language problem facing Scottish writers until an exhaustive study has been made of the language of the old anonymous folk poetry... ' Quoted in Timothy Neat, *Hamish Henderson: A Biography* (Birlinn: Edinburgh 2007), Vol. 1, p. 284.

11. 'Yiddish, the Language of Exile' in Douglas Villiers (ed.), *Next Year In Jerusalem* (Harrap: London, 1976), pp 62-63.

12. Sydney Goodsir Smith, *A Short Introduction to Scottish Literature* (Serif Books: Edinburgh, 1951) 9-10.

13. Lewis Mumford, *The City in History* (Harcourt Brace: New York, 1979) 113.

14. Quoted in Timothy Neat, *Hamish Henderson: A Biography* (Birlinn: Edinburgh, 2007), Vol. 1, p. 307.

15. I have chosen to write the Scots here much as I would recite it, or, just

as I, in fact, set it to music and recorded it with Jim Reid in the album, *Yont The Tay* (Greentrax Recordings, 2005).

16. Hamburger partly quotes and partly paraphrases Sigurd Burckhardt here. Michael Hamburger, *The Truth of Poetry* (Penguin: Harmondsworth, 1969), p. 38.

17 Lewis Grassic Gibbon, *Sunset Song* (Canongate: Edinburgh, 2006) p. 108.

18 Lewis Grassic Gibbon, *Smeddum: a Lewis Grassic Gibbon Anthology* (Canongate: Edinburgh, 2001) p. 793.

19. 'They went quiet and brave from the lands they loved, though seldom of that love might they speak , it was not in them to tell in words of the earth that moved and lived and abided, their life and enduring love.' Lewis Grassic Gibbon, *Sunset Song* (Canongate: Edinburgh, 2006) pp 255-256.

INTRODUCTION

Mary Symon's poems, notably those dealing with the First World War, are relatively well-known and often anthologised, yet have been unavailable in print for some time. The only volume of her work, *Deveron Days*, published during her lifetime (and re-issued shortly after her death) is almost impossible to find for sale, and few copies exist even in libraries.

Mary Symon was born in Dufftown, Banffshire on 25th September 1863, the elder of two daughters of Isabella Duncan and John Symon, the provost of Dufftown. Dufftown is now mostly known as one of the centres of whisky distilling in the Speyside area, and John Symon had an involvement in the distillery at Pittyvaich (now closed) where he owned an estate.

The family were generally prosperous. Mary Symon never married or left her childhood home apart from her school and university days in Edinburgh. Symon's father died in 1908 and her mother (who was incapacitated and blind and cared for by Mary for some years before her death) in 1924.[1]

Symon was educated at Mortlach public school (Dufftown was originally named Mortlach until James Duff, Fourth Earl of Fife, improved the town and it adopted his own name in the early nineteenth century) and then the Edinburgh Institute for Young Ladies and the University of Edinburgh. She was well read and began to write poetry in her teens, her first work being a poem about the completion of Mortlach Parish Church, which she attended all her life. However, she was also well versed in Dufftown local history and lore, and she is credited with writing the town guide in 1923.[2]

Symon's development as a poet, and particularly as a writer of Scottish vernacular verse, can largely be credited to two men who produced possibly the two best-known volumes of verse in Scotland around the turn of last century.

Her English teacheEdinburgh was James Logie Robertson, who, under the pen name Hugh Haliburton, produced a popular volume

of Scots verse, *Horace in Homespun*.[3] *Horace in Homespun* is probably
best known, to book buyers at least, through the memorial volume
published by Blackwood in 1925—(after Robertson's death in 1922)
with an introduction by Janet Logie Robertson, the writer's daughter—
which can still be found in countless secondhand book shops. In it, the
writer's alter ego, Hugh Haliburton, or 'Hughie', an Ochils shepherd,
reflects on life in broad Scots. In fact, these poems had appeared in
the *Scotsman* from the 1880s onwards and in the first collected volume
of 1886. Additional poems were added later and the memorial volume
ends with a long poem titled *On the Decadence of the Scots Language,
Manners, and Customs* which bemoans the decline of the Scots language,
a theme that Symon was later to refute in her poem *Oor Doric Dead!* As
well as being influenced by her interest in the Scots language, Symon's
poetic style, in the use of the first person, the Scots orthography and,
notably, of Latin quotation, may be seen as derived from Robertson.

The second influential figure was Charles Murray, born in Alford in
1864, who spent a great deal of his working life in South Africa and
served in the Boer War and the First World War before returning to
the North-east in 1924. His major volume of poetry, *Hamewith*, was
extremely popular and was first published in 1900, subsequently going
through many editions.[4]

The 1917 edition, with an introduction by Andrew Lang, was
illustrated by A S Boyd (who had also illustrated the first edition of
Horace in Homespun) and the title page featured a walker with a knapsack
and a broad colonial hat walking up a winding road to a small cottage.
Figuratively it could be Murray himself returning home.[5] Symon
corresponded with Charles Murray and, as well as appreciating his
interest in and use of the Scots language, she also sympathised with
his recurrent theme of the exile, nostalgic for the land of his birth—
the theme which, in fact, came to the fore when she created her poems
about the wartime soldier, lost in foreign lands. Symon considers this
in a manuscript note which could, in essence, have been written by
Murray himself:

I remember hearing a Rhodesian mine owner—a north-country

Scot—say that he never knew what home-love meant until one day in that faraway colony when he looked over his little boy's shoulder while the youngster was swotting over his geography lesson. He had an atlas open in front of him and the father pointed with his finger to Scotland, saying as he did so: 'that is home, my boy, where your mother and I lived, and where, please God, we shall go some day and take you with us'. The youngster looked for a minute at the spot—oh so tiny in that hemispheric infinitude—and then shrilled at him: 'well, you know, dad, if I were over there, on that little corner, I would be afraid to go out in the dark for fear I should step over the side'.[6]

One of Murray's poems, *Hame*, perhaps exemplifies this strand in his work which was to influence Symon (who, of course, seldom strayed from her own home in Dufftown):

Aft as I lie 'neath a foreign sky
In dreams I see them a'—
The auld dear kirk, the dear auld hame,
The glen sae far awa'.
Dreams flee at dawn, and the tropic sun
Nae ray o' hope can gie;
I wander on o'er the desert lone,
There's nae mair hame for me.

Similar sentiments and style can be seen in one of Symon's poems, *Hame (St Andrew's Day under the Southern Cross)*:

Ay, we are Reubens, rovers,
'Neath many an alien star,
But flaunt the blue flag o'er us,
Pipe up the 'Braes o' Mar,'

And steppe and nullah vanish,
And pomp and pelf and fame—

It's gloamin'—on a lown hillside,
   An' lads, … We're … Hame.

Murray was a continual inspiration to Symon—she claims in a manuscript note that 'Incidentally, I cannot imagine life without 'The Whistle'—'Hamewith' generally'—and, on 9th December 1929 she travelled to London to give a lecture to the Vernacular Circle of the London Burns Club entitled : 'A Modern Scottish Poet (Charles Murray, LL.D.)'.[7] In her *Burns Nicht in the Glen*, humorously, she elevates Murray to the status of the bard![8]

  …An'—bonnets aff, lads, bonnets aff—
    To hear yon 'Whistle' play.
  Oh, Robin's chair for lang's been teem,
    Lat Charlie tak' it noo—
  An' twine the heather an' the breem—
    A laurel for his broo.

Interestingly, the contention at that time that Murray was a 'modern' Scottish poet was not accepted by the Scottish literary establishment in its entirety. Symon's poems had come to the attention of Hugh MacDiarmid, then using his birth name of Christopher Murray Grieve,[9] and he published three of them in his edited collection of new Scottish literature, *Northern Numbers*.[10] The first series of *Northern Numbers* had been published by the Foulis Press in 1920 and contained the work of eleven poets—Violet Jacob being the most notable North -easterner. The second series followed in 1921[11] and the contributors were expanded to nineteen, including Symon and Charles Murray.

Grieve allowed the poets to choose their own representative works and Symon is represented by *The Echt-Day Clock*, *The Soldiers' Cairn* and *Hame (St Andrew's Day under the Southern Cross)*. These can be seen as representative of the three strands of her work: vernacular poetry of everyday life, war poetry, and the almost elegiac strain of the exile in her more meditative poems.

Symon corresponded with MacDiarmid and he notes in a letter

dated 29th December 1921: 'The second edition of *Northern Numbers* is going well and has been praised by various poets. Miss Symon says 'Your things are powerful—very' and intimates that on the strength of their appeal she has ordered a copy of Annals…'[12]

At this time, however, MacDiarmid was nurturing some objections to forms of Scottish vernacular poetry. The main object of MacDiarmid's ire lay not in Scotland, but in England, with a group called The Vernacular Circle within the London Burns Club, the same group that had hosted Symon's lecture on Murray.[13] Strangely, two Scots from the North-east who were both journalists, both confidants of Symon—and who both, coincidently, became editors of the magazine *The Graphic* (edited from Whitefriars, London)—were instrumental in the founding of this group. They were William Will and John Malcolm Bulloch.

William Will was from Strathbogie, the hinterland of the town now called Huntly, home of the Gordon Highlanders and barely ten miles from Dufftown. He lived until 1956 and The Burns Club of London still stages a William Will Memorial Lecture. Some of the correspondence between Will and Symon is preserved in the National Library of Scotland.[14] It seems that Will first wrote to Symon in 1919 (before the publication of *Northern Numbers*) asking about her Scots poems. She replied on 10th May 1919 stressing the importance of the Scots tongue in an educational context:[15] 'The educational or, at any rate, school aegis in the vernacular is a capital idea… In recent schoolbooks there are one or two Doric selections among the English verse but they are, for the most part, badly chosen, while the glossaries are absolutely inadequate.' In the eighteenth century, Doric was the term commonly applied to all Scots usage. It is derived from a classical reference; a rustic style preferred by the pastoral poet Theocritus in opposition to the classical Roman style (Doria was a rural area near Sparta). Later it tends to mean northern or north-eastern Scots. More recently it is usually taken to refer to the vernacular Scots of the North-east of Scotland alone and Lallans is a term employed referring to the speech used in the lowlands areas of Scotland, as opposed to the Highlands, where Gaelic was traditionally spoken. Lallans also refers to the

Borders area of Scotland, where the term Doric is seldom employed. Scots is the term largely employed in serious literature today.[16]

Perhaps enthused by this, Will proposed the formation of a Vernacular Circle to the Burns Club on 7th June 1920 and an extract from the minutes indicates that he was supported by Mary Symon: 'Miss Mary Symon of Dufftown, one of our foremost Scottish poetesses, has written repeatedly to me urging upon the London Burns Club the desirability of taking action'. In fact, a letter from Mary Symon to William Will of 19th October 1920 encloses a cheque donating £5 to the Circle. Subsequently, on 22nd November 1920, Will gave the first lecture to the Circle entitled 'The Preservation of the Scottish Vernacular'. The Circle continued to develop over the next few years. Honorary members included not only Mary Symon, but also Violet Jacob, Charles Murray and James Logie Robertson. A lecture of 11th March 1921 by John Douglas entitled 'New and Old Vernacular Poets of Scotland' used Symon, Jacob and Murray as examples.[17]

On 12th December 1921, John Malcolm Bulloch delivered a paper entitled 'The Delight of the Doric in the Diminutive' to the Vernacular Circle. The gist of the lecture was that the diminutive form was common in Scots but not in English in general. Therefore, in Scots description, the emphasis in description is on small, or limited, or unimportant. 'Wee' is a keystone word. He moots a couple of contentious reasons for this (Scots feel small as a result of our struggle with elements such as the sea, or in the face of a rigid Calvinist God) but the more cogent argument as to the location of the diminutive in the Scot's psychology he takes from Symon who is praised excessively: 'Miss Symon is not only a constructive artist of a very high quality, but she is an extraordinarily incisive critic of our psychology, and a past master of our most distinctive Doric, and of all the people I have canvassed she has flashed by far the most brilliant beam of understanding. Here is her contribution:

> Diminutives are our only emotional outlets. We have practically no endearments. The southerner spreads himself out on 'dears,' 'darlings,' 'beloveds' and such-like saccharinities. The tidal wave of passion swamps the Scot. Even the mildest of ordinary, everyday

loves remain unexpressed either directly or indirectly because there is no vocabulary for them. It is somebody of Barrie's, I think, who says: 'Love ye? Wheest! Fat kin' o' a word's that to be makin' eese o'—an' fowk a' well eneuch'. In a vague unformulated fashion we consider tenderness a weakness, very nearly an indecency. At any rate we fight shy of it. We are shy of it. 'Love, but dinna lat on' about sums up all the erotic philosophy of the hill plaid and the sleeved weskit. So in our soft moments—no dithryrambics, no little urbanites, or amiabilities. We just drop into diminutives.[18]

MacDiarmid, however, at this stage of his career, had taken exception to the dialect poetry of the North-east which he was beginning to see as too entwined in a sentimental, insular and parochial tradition associated with the Burns cult which he saw as detrimental to the development of Scots as a modern literary language. He was to develop what is often called a synthetic (or 'plastic', by his detractors) Scots that could be applied to the whole of modern Scotland.[19] This is expressed in a letter to the *Aberdeen Free Press* written on 13th December 1921 and printed two days later in which he states that 'Dr Bulloch's plea for Doric infanitism is only worthy of the critical consideration of nursery-governesses... Miss Symon's opinions I respect: but her views of Scottish psychology have been determined geographically. If she lived in Lanarkshire or West Fife she would know that the processes of evolution have carried the most important sections of the Scottish nation far beyond the hill-plaid and 'sleevid weskit' stage.'[20]

In fact, it was not only Bulloch, but the members of the London/Scots literary establishment in general that MacDiarmid took exception to. They were well-off, English and, from his view, lost in a sentimentalised and out-dated vision of Scotland:

The leaders of the London Vernacular Circle (who are wealthier than nine-tenths of the poets and prose writers of Scotland from Dunbar to Burns put together) are doing nothing to help such efforts as are being made in in various quarters to revive Braid Scots as an instrument of literary expression... The Doric will only revive if the very opposite spirit to them can be brought to bear and it can be made a fit medium for all-round expression of the modern Scottish mind.[21]

Symon, however, was to continue to support the Vernacular Circle and had, it seems, no other dealings with MacDiarmid. Her use of the Scots language was rooted in a wider and international appreciation of literature. She was well-read and her letters not only reveal her enthusiasm for Stevenson, Scott and Byron but for women writers of the time: Juliet Sockie (Hueffer), who wrote *Chapter from Childhood*, and Lady Margaret Sackville, who she absolves from any accusation of Anglicisation: '...but—LMS! Fiech! Never! [her writing] reeks of heather and whin, of robustious rusticity generally!'[22] She delighted in the reproduction, and probably enunciation, of local dialect words, some quite obscure even to Scots language enthusiasts today, as can be seen in this example from *Oor Doric Dead!*:

There's sneeters, footers, shargars, sclypes,
Gaun stoufin' by the door;
We're gettin' amscachs, dirds an' dunts,
But aye we tchyawe awa...

Or in this example from a rare piece of prose by Symon in which the dialogue is supposedly based on a shopkeeper in Dufftown: 'Ay, here's me, sellin' trappin' an' traikle, an' preens and pearl barley... forbye's I could dance the backstep on a peat! Well, loom, ony ither thing till your traikle rin?' or 'Fair oot, an' furth the gait, I am... If onybody's expeckin' mim-mowed slaverin' wi' their tipenny ha'penny trok—they needna come to my shop for't.'[23] In the best of her poetry of domestic life, the effective use of local dialect conjures up local characters effectively:

See, here's the bridegroom, Kirsty,
    I ken him by his breeks,

His chumley-hat and dickey,

An' the way he bobs an' keeks
Like a hen that's heark'nin' thunner,
   Or a corbie seekin' 's hole,
He'll be mirkier at his burial
   Tho' he winna look as droll.

Of course, there is a paradox here. Despite the implied claim that her Scots is based on naturalistic speech in turn based on her everyday experience, Symon's poetic Scots—whilst not the 'synthetic' Scots of MacDiarmid—is clearly constructed for its purpose and employs different registers and vocabularies to suit her purpose. Also, two aspects of Symon's work which are fairly obvious but important should be stated here. Firstly, Symon did not speak in the Scots she employs in her writing, nor did most of the other North-eastern poets of the time (Charles Murray, Violet Jacob, Marion Angus—the exception perhaps being Flora Garry who was brought up on a farm). Symon corresponded with Violet Jacob in the twenties. She notes in a letter of 23rd November 1921 to Will: 'For I am come of a long, stainless (more or less) line of saddlers!!! *Per Contra*, look at Violet Jacob—a Kennedy-Erskine, a great grand-daughter of William IV and Mrs Fitzclarence! There's something to weep on your weskit for—eh? But when and how did she, at that altitude, acquire her bothy Gothic?'[24]

Perhaps this is meant tongue-in-cheek, but it begs fair the question—from whence does the Doric voice in poetry of the North-east derive? It certainly does not come from everyday speakers of broad Scots, and neither Violet Jacob nor Mary Symon are likely to have spoken it in their everyday lives. Similarly, the gentlemen of the Vernacular Circle were generally wealthy businessmen—mostly based in London. The enthusiasm for the vernacular in one way can be seen as fuelled by a middle-class nostalgia for a working-class lifestyle. Yet the interest of many of the North-east poets in Scots was engendered by an everyday experience of spoken Scots. As Kathleen Gordon points out, 'For [Marion] Angus and [Violet] Jacob, using Scots was an overtly political statement as it was for MacDiarmid.'[25]

Secondly, Symon, in common with other North-east poets, did not write alone in Scots. She stresses her preference for Scots as a poetic

medium—'Oh, English speech for English yird!/ We ken it's granda'
fine:/ But ah! it tak's the dear Scots word/ To grip your heart an'
mine'—but is happy to also write in English and a hybrid of English
and Scots (and even Cockney, as in *Bill Smith's Chum Says*) when the
occasion calls for it. She is also happy to introduce Latin and words
derived from various languages.

Some of her poems are entirely in conventional English but, more
importantly, she uses a mixture of local Moray Scots, more general
Scots and conventional English in her work. In fact, some of the
most powerful lines of her poems use different forms of language
to contrast, perhaps, the local and the universal, or an individual and
generic voice. J D McClure notes that 'Mary Symon's use of her local
Doric is, in fact, a carefully-controlled artistic tool'.[26] He employs the
example of *A Recruit for the Gordons* to demonstrate this: The first half
of the stanza contains no fewer than four local dialect features: the
expression eat-meat (an idler or parasite), the special sense skyte (here
meaning a drink), the word quine and the pronunciation Eel. The
second half, none at all, all the Scots features being common to the
whole Scots-speaking area. The suggestion of a light-hearted ferm-
loon consciously transforming himself into a dedicated soldier, and
aware of the somewhat ludicrous contrast between what he has been
and what he is awkwardly but sincerely trying to become, is suggested
with delicacy and poignancy by the change in language.[27]

Mary Symon used language creatively and could move from specific
local dialect, through more general Scots to standard English to a
mixed vernacular. However, her primary focus and the force behind
her best poems was the local dialect which surrounded her and this
applied in general to the poets of the North-east. As Colin Milton
points out:

One important stimulus to the literary use of regional Scots was local
patriotism; writers with particular regional loyalties were moved, in
Scotland and elsewhere, to resist the powerful contemporary forces
making for a cultural standardisation. It was an impulse which had
more than a parochial importance. Developments in the North-east
can be seen as part of that general attempt, which gathered strength

among progressive writers in the second half of the last century,
to escape from a literary idiom which had become banal, inert and
archaic—the aim was to 'wring the neck of rhetoric', in Verlaine's
famous phrase, and forge a vigorous and contemporary literary
medium. Writers became interested in the spoken rather than the
written word, in the popular, non-standard and even 'disreputable'
forms of language—in class and regional dialects, in slang and cant,
as well as in specialist and technical vocabularies of all sorts. It
might seem far-fetched to link Verlaine and Charles Murray, but in
some ways they were both part of the same movement.[28]

Certainly, Symon's poetry and other Scots poetry of the period
derives from the spoken word, but literary Scots has a more complex
relationship with the spoken word. MacDiarmid's slogan for his
development of synthetic Scots was 'Back to Dunbar', suggesting that
the Scots of the medieval Scots poets, the 'Makars', was a more fitting
model for contemporary poets than the parochial Scots of Burns.
However, this reminds us that the Scots of the Makars was also a
constructed Scots. The entire Scots literary tradition has a fruitful but
inexact relationship with spoken Scots. There is no doubt, also, that
the North-east poets were influenced not only by local speech but also
the Scots literary tradition and vibrant folk tradition of the area, and
by 'ballad Scots'.

If local dialect, other forms of Scots and the folk tradition provided
the inspiration for the form of Symon's poetry, it was the effect of the
most traumatic event of her lifetime, the First World War, on her locality
that gave her most powerful subject matter. At the commencement of
the First World War, Charles Murray evokes its coming in the North-
east with a sigh rather than a cry:

The corn was turnin', hairst was near,
But lang afore the scythes could start
A sough o' war gaed through the land...[29]

The war was to focus Symon's writing for the next few years and inspire the finest of her poems. Yvonne McEwen suggests that there was some ambiguity in her approach: '…her conflicting responses to the war can be traced in her poetry, published in magazines and newspapers of the time, from drum-beating exhortations to elegiac pieces which convey the enduring heartbreak of a nation.'[30] This is true to an extent. However, a scrutiny of her War poems also seems to reveal a uniformity both in theme and technique.

The battle of Neuve Chapelle resulted in ten thousand plus casualties only seven months after the start of the War[31] and Symon evokes the aftermath in *After Neuve Chapelle* with what seems a call to arms:

> Oh, glens that gave the Gordons, is't you will give as well
> The cohorts of the damned and done that heed nae
> > Neuve Chapelle?
> God! Will they ever wauken, the loons that sit at hame?
> While din-faced Sikhs an' Ghurkas
> Fecht to keep oor shores fae shame.
> Oor kin fae a' the Seven Seas are tummelin' to the fray
> But there's laggards yet on lown hillsides 'neath skies that
> > span the Spey…

Yet in A *Recruit for the Gordons*, she employs a lighter, almost humorous, touch to portray a innocent young lad called to the War:

> Ay me! 'At never shot a craw,
> > Nor killed a cushey-doo—
> But bleed's aye bleed, an' aul granda
> > Did things at Waterloo.
> I'm aff the morn…There's nane'll ken
> > O' ae broon curly head,
> That ees't to lie aside my ain
> > In Mains's stoupet bed.
> It's laich, laich noo, in Flanders sod,
> > An' I'm mairchin' wi' the drum,
> 'Cause doon the lang La Bassée road
> > There's dead lips cryin' 'Come!'

Some critics have expressed the view that this poem 'doesn't question conventional constructions of heroism'.[32] Yet the notable change of voice in the last line gives the poem a poignancy and a more serious purpose. Unfortunately, we cannot be absolutely sure of the order in which Symon wrote her War poems, but it seems likely that the cumulative reports of casualties from the Front may have led to a more thoughtful and elegiac appoach to Symon's writing.

The development of the War was, in fact, to have a devasting effect throughout Scotland, but was expecially intense in Symon's own Morayshire parish, the Cabrach, as noted by Norman Harper:

As any self-respecting North-easterner knows, The Cabrach is Scotland's obvious testament to the waste of young life in wartime. The great numbers of tumbledown crofts and steadings you see in that triangle bounded by Dufftown, Rhynie and Lumsden happened not because of land policy or the Depression or a series of bad farming years. They happened because virtually all the fighting-age men and boys went off to war in 1914. Many did not return...They believed politicians and newspaper leader-writers who said that the more men who joined up, and the quicker they did it, the sooner the enemy would be defeated and the earlier they could be home. It was the original 'home by Christmas'. We all know now that it didn't happen that way. Many died either in battle or because they succumbed to measles, to which they had no immunity because they came from such a self-contained community... The women, children and old folk they had left behind to keep the crofts ticking over for the implied four months could not survive beyond a second Cabrach winter and eventually had to find accommodation and work elsewhere. They abandoned the crofts, and what you see a century later was once described by a Dutch academic historian as 'the biggest war memorial in Europe'.[33]

Symon's response to this carnage is one of her finest poems: *The Glen's Muster-Roll.* This poem was published in the *Aberdeen University Review* in February 1916 just before the Battle of the Somme.[34] The substance of the poem is the local dominie's recounting of the muster roll (or roster) of the names of his pupils who have perished in the War:

> Hing't up aside the chumley-cheek, the aul' glen's
>   Muster Roll,
> A' names we ken fae hut an' ha', fae Penang to the Pole,
> An' speir na gin I'm prood o't—losh! coont them
>   line by line,
> Near han' a hunner fechtin' men, an' they a' were
>   Loons o' Mine.

The personalities of the various pupils are detailed: Sandy, Dick, Tam, the Gaup, Davie and Robbie, the most academic, whose fate is not to perish but to come 'hirplin' hame' a cripple. The last verse imagines them all returning in a vision, now not 'lauchin' loons' but 'hell-scarred' men questioning their master regarding the meaning of what has happened, to which he has no reply:

> My Loons, my Loons! Yon winnock gets the settin' sun
>   the same,
> Here's sklates and skailies, ilka dask a' futtled wi' a name.
> An' as I sit a vision comes: Ye're troopin' in aince mair,
> Ye're back fae Aisne an' Marne an' Meuse, Ypres an' Festubert;
> Ye're back on weary bleedin' feet—you, you that danced
>   an' ran—
> For every lauchin' loon I kent I see a hell-scarred man.
> Not mine but yours to question now! You lift unhappy eyes—
> 'Ah, Maister, tell's fat a' this means'.
> And I, ye thocht sae wise,
> Maun answer wi' the bairn words ye said tae me langsyne:
>   'I dinna ken, I dinna ken. Fa does, oh, Loons o' Mine.'

As J D McClure notes, '…the almost unbearable sadness of the conclusion is suggested by the very ordinariness of the language. The unexpected English line 'Not mine but yours to question now! You lift unhappy eyes'—serves simply to emphasise the heart-touching familiarity of the immediately resumed dialect'.[35]

In this poem, as in her work in general, Symon takes the local and particular and invests in it a more universal meaning. Trevor Royle notes that 'In her long poem, *The Glen's Muster-Roll*, Mary Symon extended that sense of personal loss to other rural communities which had been touched by the carnage of war. In that respect, her poem, though rooted in a community which she knew well, attains a universiality of feeling through the dominie's articulation of his personal sorrow'.[36] Leslie Wheeler notes 'Her war poetry was a poetry of genuine understanding and sympathy without crass jingoistic posturing or over-sentimental rhetoric... only in a few works will one find the sheer awfulness and horror of war more simply, but impressingly, portrayed than in the touching litany of *The Glen's Muster Roll* – the carnage of the glen's youth being mirrored in countless parishes throughout the country.'[37]

The Soldiers' Cairn concerns the building of a cairn to the casualties of the war, a practice that, of course, was not only particular to the Cabrach, but to parishes throughout Scotland. The first verse either directly addresses the builders of the cairn or, perhaps more poignantly, addresses the dead soldiers who are being honoured from the hill chosen for the cairn—'(D'ye mind on't, Will? Are ye hearin', Dod?)'—while the second shifts to Flanders where they lie in '...a hap o' the Gordon green.' The third verse develops the theme:

Doon, laich doon the Dullan sings—
    An' I ken o' an aul' sauch tree,
Where a wee loon's wahnie's hingin' yet
    That's dead in Picardy;
An' ilka win' fae the Conval's broo
    Bends aye the buss o' ern,
Where aince he futtled a name that noo
    I'll read on the Soldiers' Cairn.

The comparison between the local and the foreign (fremmit) lands to which the dead are exiled is now elaborated on by a counterpoint between the living and the dead, the present and the past. So the wind blows the branch of a tree on which the 'wee loon' has whittled his name. Now his name is to be permanently inscribed on the cairn.

Subsequently, Symon turns to standard English to move from the specific to the general and the universal and to suggest that the cairn isn't just a symbol of the past but a lesson for the future, with the cairn itself developing a new importance as 'a new earth's cornerstone':

> More, more than death is symbolled there,
>   Than tears or triumphs by.
> There's the Dream Divine of a starward way
>   Oor laggard feet would learn—
> It's a new earth's corner-stone we'd lay
>   As we fashion the Soldiers' Cairn.

The final verse, however, moves back to the specific and combines the themes of the poem in a poignant and powerful climax.

> Lads in your plaidies lyin' still,
>   In lands we'll never see,
> This lanely cairn on a hameland hill
>   Is a' that oor love can dee;
> An' fine an' braw we'll mak' it a',
>   *But oh, my Bairn, my Bairn,*
> *It's a cradle's croon that'll aye blaw doon*
>   *To me fae the Soldiers' Cairn.*

The voice moves from a generic lament for all the dead to a specific case, the mother's lament for her lost child. This is reminiscent of one of MacDiarmid's early lyric poems, *Empty Vessel*. [38]

MacDiarmid may have regarded the poetry of Symon and some of her contemporaries as sentimental and parochial, but such a charge cannot be laid against *The Soldiers' Cairn*, perhaps the finest of her poems. A contemporary and considered mix of Scots and English moves from pathos to a universal vision which concludes with an unexpected and powerful evocation of a mother and child which provides a metaphoric link between the tragedy of the past and hope for the future. Women's poetry of the First World War has been described as twofold: dealing with both a personal and public grief[39] and this is exemplified here. Fred Freeman analyses this particular poem in more detail in the preface to this volume. However, this poem alone surely contradicts absolutely the statement of one critic that 'Garry and Symon are ultimately minor figures, similar to but far outshone by Jacob and Angus'.[40]

Perhaps the strangest of Symon's war poems, published here for the first time, is *Bill Smith's Chum Says*.[41] This work focuses on the practice of gathering sphagnum moss, which was shipped to the war to be employed in dressing wounds.[42] The first component metaphor of this work, therefore, is of the land, the locality, figuratively acting as a cure for the horrors of the war. Secondly, however, another meaning becomes clear:

> … Oh, yes, It's the moss we're doin',
> But, by gum, the moss ain't all.
> There's a mighty lot o' thinkin'
> Been done in this 'ere hall.
> Why, folks as were hardly speakin'
> An' hating each other like mad,
> Jest over the moor has been lovin' and kind,
> As they think o' some soldier lad
> Who's fightin' away out yonder,
> Fightin' for Earth's Big Things
> An' makin' them sick ashamed o' sulks
> An' swappin' digs an' flings.
> … ay, I think we're growing better,
> Kinder and straighter too,
> An' it's all along o' the moss, you know,
> An' soldier lads o' you.

Both the practice of actually gathering the moss, therefore, and the practice of musing on the trials and tribulations of the soldiers, acts as a metaphoric cure for the community and a sort of scourging of the ills therein, as in *Wir Roup*, written near the end of the War and more a an observation of local culture than a comment on the War:

> An' Sodger Lad, when oor wee bit
>   Gangs owre the sea to you,
> Will ye hear the win' at your ain brae-fit
>   An' the burnie soughin' through?

> Will ye hear the whaup on the hills again?
>   But abeen them a, my dear,
> There's a voice o' love fae yer ain fire-en'
>   That we'd like ye best to hear.

This theme of the healing power of not just the substance of the land but also, indeed, the *memory* of it, recurs in Symon's work as, for example, in *A Whiff o' Hame*. In fact, the word 'hame' (or occasionally 'home') appears no fewer than 54 times in her poems (three times in the titles). This is true not only of the war poems but of the poems of domestic life and the more meditative poems. In *The Wag-At-The-Wa'* it is the ticking of the old clock that figuratively reaches out to exiles in the far corners of the world:

> Ay, we're a' scattered noo, but it's aye tickin' on—
> Ye hear't at the dykeside, ye hear't up the loan—
> Ye hear't—divn't ye, lad? by the lang lippin' seas
> That soom by yir doorcheek at the Antipodes.
> An' Tam, wi' yir tackets on Ottawa's steep,
> What is't that comes hack when ye canna get sleep?
> Jist the croon o' a burn in a far-awa' glen,
> The clink o' a churn, or a fit comin' ben,
> An' in laich obligato, the lift an' the fa',
> The sab an' the sang o' a Wag-at-the-wa'.

The meditative poems that make up the final section of this collection are suffused with a strong sense of homeland that moves beyond patriotism, through nostalgia to the quasi-spiritual in which the narrator's (usually childhood) home is expressed in almost mystical terms—'dear land o' memory' (*An Appeal*); 'a house o' memory', 'land of yesterday' (*From the East*)—as a sort of lost Tir-nan-Og. Throughout her poetry, interestingly, Symon primarily employs a neutral or a male voice, but in a couple of the meditative poems about death—*From the East* and *In Appin*—the voice is female and there is a simplicity of style more akin to the folk or ballad tradition:

But we'll baith win back to Appin—
   Some day the sun'll shine
An' the same saft rain be drappin'
   On your grave as on mine.
When there's naithing mair'll pairt us
   Than a strip o kirkyard green—
Ay, Death, lad, will be kinder till's
   Than ever Life has been—
An' it's lythe we'll lie in Appin,
   When the lang day's deen.

The last verse of *The End* is similar, and these poems bear comparison with one of Violet Jacobs's best known poems *The Last o the Tinkler:*

Ye'll rise to meet the sun, lad,
An baith be traivelin' west,
But me that's auld and duin, lad,
I'll bide and tak my rest,
For the grey heid is bendin',
An the auld shuins needin' mendin'
But the traivelin's near it's endin,
And the end's aye the best.

This poem also became a popular song. However, most of Symon's poetry is too complex in form to be set to music. One exception is

The Soldiers' Cairn, which has been set to a tune by Fred Freeman and recorded by the folksinger Jim Reid on the album *Yont the Tay* with the title *The Sodgers Cairn*.

In general, however, the meditations on home and the nature of home constitute the most enduring theme of Symon's work.

> It's Hame, it's Hame for ever,
> Let good or ill betide!
> The croon o' some dear river,
> The blink o' ae braeside.

The main oppositions in her work centre on distance, home and abroad, and the passage from life to death. However, the trauma that emanates in a literary trope occurs when the passage through life to old age and death is broken by the onset of the war and the death of the young. This is exemplified by the contrast in *The Glen's Muster-Roll* between the schoolmaster and the children. Only in *The Auld Fisher*, perhaps, is a more natural or tranquil passage through life evoked:

> I've had my pridefu' meenits
>   In my lang pilgrimage,
> But when a' is said and deen—it's
>   Could I turn back Life's page.
> I'd tak' ae bonnie mornin'
>   Wi' the sun on lea an' hill,
> An' the soun' o water churnin'
>   Roun' the clapper o' a mill.

William Will, it seems, had first suggested publishing a volume of Symon's poems in late 1919. Previously, they had appeared in various periodicals and some had been distributed as pamphlets.[43] On 3rd October 1920, Will writes 'have you got those 'bitties' thegither yet?' and adds: 'I have had another letter from Charles Murray in which he says he is glad you have at last committed to publish.' On St Andrew's Day, 1921 Will writes suggesting a publisher: Macniven & Wallace, of

Princes Street, Edinburgh. Subsequently, on 20th July 1922, Foulis and Constable is mentioned.[44]

Her poems were eventually published in 1933 under the title *Deveron Days* by D Wylie & Son, a small but noted publisher in Aberdeen.[45] The book was dedicated to 'That Scot of Scots William Will'—a then famous journalist and 'illustrious son of Strathbogie'. The title had been used for pieces in *The Scots Magazine* in 1925 but it seems it was originally conceived by William Will as a title for the book as she notes in an undated letter to him: 'I never thought of 'Deveron Days'. The only point for the 'Days' is the illiteration.' The first impression was released in December 1933 and more than three hundred copies sold out immediately. A second impression was released in January 1934. Symon noted in a letter that its success 'sounds grand indeed!' Presumably its fame spread widely as she received, on 6th July 1934, a letter praising the book from the treasurer of New York City.[46] A second edition of *Deveron Days* was published in 1938 shortly after Mary Symon's death.

The success of *Deveron Days* brought her to the attention of Robert Gordon's Academy, and she was requested to write a school song which she duly did. It was sung at the end of Scene V, Act II of a play called *The Auld Hoose*, performed on Founders Day, 1934.[47] The title was *For We're a' Gordonians Here*:

Out from the vaulted gateway,
    With the march of eager feet,
The lads of the laughing legions
    Fare forth the world to meet;
The world to meet and master –
    O wizardry benign!
Omni nunc arte magistra
    Sings in your heart and mine

    Chorus:
    For we're a' Gordonians here,
    We're a' Gordonians here,

Tho' far and lang
The road we gang,
There's ae bield where we a' belang,
The bield we'll aye hold dear.

We are the lads of Gordon's,
    And Gordon's aye we'll be
Whate'er the fates we follow,
    Whate'er the lands we see.
On soldier, sage or toiler
    The olden glamour falls—
We're sons to greet a mother,
    Within these storied walls
Set in yon stately city,
    O school of memory,
All winds of the world are wafting
    Our dream-thoughts back to thee,
Where aye the turf is green, lads,
    And youth will clarion still,
And the morning stars be shining
    Above the old Schoolhill.

Mary Symon died at her home, Pittyvaich House, on 27th May 1938. She was buried alongside her parents in the cemetery at Mortlach Old Church and the pall bearers included Charles Murray. Her wealth at death was recorded as £338 16s 1d. In one of her letters to William Will (written seventeen years before her death) she notes 'Of old I had one simple and yet soaring ambition—this—that when I go hence, I should have 'she was a cheery craitur' carved on my tombstone'.[48] In one of her translations from the French poet Beranger, *The Cheery Chiel*, the eponymour chiel is contrasted with the dour village folk:

He fiddled, diddled, danced awa',
    Fae parischen to toon;

Newsed i' the neuk wi' aul' gran'da,
  Furled totums wi' the loon.
Laughter and Love—the kingly wares
  He cairriet in his creel—
He niffer't for oor sabs an' sairs,
  The Cheery Chapman Chiel.

The *Dufftown News* in an obituary described her as follows: 'She was a woman of extraordinarily wide culture, familiar with several languages and a keen and discerning student of literature, philosophy and life. Old Scottish words and phrases were constantly on her lips when she was in the company of those who understood the charm of the pure vernacular. Her native countryside and its people and customs she loved with a passionate devotion.'

Her work is of various quality with both her prose and poetry occasionally tending towards a sort of linguistic virtuosity that at its worst verges on tautology or even obscurity.[49] However, the best of her verse is enduring as evidenced by the popularity of, for example, *The Soldiers' Cairn*. The first of her major poems of the First World War was written at the age of 52 and the first published collection of her poems appeared when she was 70. Death is figuratively evoked in her poem *The End*:

Jist lift me to the winnock, lass,
  An' lay me canny doon;
I'd like to see the sun again
  Set fair owre field an' toon.
I'm gaun awa' to leave them a',
  On a journey lane an' lang;
But Death has ca'ed fu' kindly,
  An' I'm no' that sweer to gang.

It's jist like fa'in' asleep, lass,
  An' a' my trauchle deen,
To rest my tired bit hannies,

An' steek my weary een;
To never thole the ruggin' hert,
  The tchave, the fecht the din,
To never hear the bairnies greet
  For bread I canna win.

It's jist like waukenin' up, lass,
  An' the mornin' brakin' fine
On the lang, lane glints o' heather,
  In a glen I kent lang syne;
Wi' the lave rock singin' bonnie
  In a lift that's lown an' blue,
An' father waitin' at the yett,
  Sayin' 'Jeanie, this is you.'

This volume is titled *Collected Poems* but it cannot in any way claim to be the *complete* collected poems of Mary Symon. Although the editors have endeavoured to locate as many poems as is practical, Symon's habit of writing under various pseudonyms for a variety of publications and the relative lack of manuscript copies of her work means that there may be several other poems to be found and identified. One poem found in the manuscript written in her hand is *Granny's Cradle*. A note attributes this to 'La Teste' or William Tester, an Aberdeenshire poet known for a collection of Victorian sentimental verse. But he wrote mostly in standard English, and this is untypical of his style, that that seems unlikely. So, possibly, it is an unacknowledged production of Symon herself.[50]

As to the orthography of the poems, the few surviving manuscript copies suggest that Symon wrote her verse in long single lines which subsequent editors have truncated to fit the page. This is also the case in this volume although the divisions have been chosen as carefully as possible to maintain the rhythm of the verse.

Ian Spring

NOTES

1. The best short summary of her life can be found at http:/www.morayconnections.com.

2. *Dufftown: Official Town Guide* (1923).

3. Hugh Haliburton, *Horace in Homespun*. A series of Scottish pastorals, with preface, notes, and glossary by J Logie Robertson, MA (privately printed: Edinburgh, 1886).

4. Charles Murray, *Hamewith* (D Wylie & Son: Aberdeen, 1900).

5. Charles Murray, *Hamewith* (Constable & Co: London, 1917).

6. National Library of Scotland manuscript sources for Mary Symon are Acc 3501 5, Acc 7534 2.

7. Mitchell Library: ML No. 898054. Poems by Murray read to the meeting (not by Symon) included *Still, Man, Still, A Green Yule, The Glen is Mine* and *Bydand*. Symon also gave a lecture on Murray to the U F Dramatic & Literary Society as recorded in the *Banffshire Journal* (29th February 1929).

8. Neither of Symon's main influences have maintained their early reputation. For example: 'Haliburton's version of Horation odes... often smacked of the patronising literary exercise... [Murray] never penetrated the secret places of the heart or the subtler intricacies of the intellect... his style... was often prosaic and he tended to look towards the past.' Alexander Scott, 'Hugh MacDiarmid and the Scots Tradition' in *Hugh MacDiarmid: A Critical Survey*, Edinburgh: Scottish Academic Press, 1972, pp 1-11, pp 7-8.

9. Referred to in this introduction as Hugh MacDiarmid to avoid confusion.

10. *Northern Numbers* (T N Foulis: Edinburgh, 1920) and *Northern Numbers* (T N Foulis: Edinburgh, 1921).

11. *Northern Numbers* (T N Foulis: Edinburgh, 1920), pp 123-128.

12.. Hugh MacDiarmid, *New Selected Letters* (Carcanet Press: Manchester, 2001), p. 69. The book referred to is Hugh MacDiarmid, *Annals of the Five Senses* (C M Grieve: Montrose, 1923).

13. The London Burns Club was founded in 1868 at the behest of Colin Rae Brown, a wealthy newspaper proprietor originally from Greenock. Many notable persons present at the first meeting included the engraver George Cruickshank and Charles Mackay, the Perth-born author of *Extraordinary Popular Delusions and the Madness of Crowds*, who became a president of the club. In 1921, the club merged with another club that had been founded in London and the name was altered slightly to The Burns Club of London. William Will wrote a history of the club. William Will, *Burns Club of London* (J & J Gray: Edinburgh, 1938).

14. This and subsequent quotations from the letters between Mary Symon and William Will come from the National Library of Scotland manuscript. Acc 3501 5.

15. The Vernacular Circle sponsored a number of awards to promote Scots in schools.

16. Contemporary definitions of Scots have been compounded by the practice of the Scots Language Centre to refer to any dialect of the Scottish language (Shetlandic, Glaswegian, etc) as Scots.

17. The minutes of the Club are partially preserved in the Mitchell Library: ML No. 898054 Burns Club of London, Vernacular Circle: Minutes 1920-21, 1923-29. Other lectures included Colonel John Buchan, 'Some Scottish Characteristics', 7th February 1921, and W A Craigie, MA, LL D., Professor of Anglo-Saxon at Oxford University, 'The Present State of the Scottish Tongue'.

18. W A Craigie, *The Scots Tongue: a series of lectures on the vernacular language of lowland Scotland* (Cassell & Co: London, 1924), pp 143-44. William Will notes in the foreword: ' ...having viewed the danger ahead, The Burns Club of London in 1920 formed the Vernacular Circle to devise a method of preserving from entire destruction the language in which the mentality of the lowland Scot can best be expressed'. For a discussion on Symon's statement on diminutives see also, Carol Craig, *The Scots' Crisis of Confidence* (Big Thinking: Glasgow, 2003), p. 71.

19. Douglas Young, *Plastic Scots and the Scottish Literary Tradition* (William Maclellan: Glasgow, 1948).

20. Hugh MacDiarmid, *New Selected Letters* (Carcanet Press: Manchester, 2001), pp 750-751. Regarding this also see Alan Bold, *MacDiarmid* (Paladin: London, 1988), pp 148-149.

21. C M Grieve 'Contemporary Scottish Studies', *Scottish Education Journal* (5th February, 1926) makes a plea for synthetic Scots.

22. ACC 7534 2 [9th November 1921].

23. Mary Symon, 'Deveron Days: II—The Shoppie', *The Scots Magazine*, (April-September, 1928), 341-343.

24. ACC 7534 2 2.

25. Kathleen Gordon, *Voices from Their Ain Countrie: the poems of Marion Angus and Violet Jacob* (Glasgow: Association for Scottish Literary Studies, 2006), p. 1.

26. J D McClure, 'Lallans' and 'Doric' in North-eastern Scottish Poetry' in *English World-Wide*, 8, 2 (1987, 215-234, p. 43.

27. J D McClure, ''Lallans' and 'Doric' in North-eastern Scottish Poetry' in

English World-Wide, 8, 2 (1987, 215-234, p. 42.

28. Colin Milton, 'A Sough o' War: The Great War in the Poetry of North-east Scotland' in David Hewitt (ed.), *Northern Visions* (East Linton: Tuckwell Press, 1985) pp 211-212.

29. Charles Murray, *Hamewith* (Constable & Co: London, 1917).

30. Lizzie MacGregor (ed.) *Beneath Troubled Skies: Poems of Scotland at War 1914-1918* (Edinburgh: Polygon, 2015), p. 148.

31. See Lizzie MacGregor (ed.) *Beneath Troubled Skies: Poems of Scotland at War 1914-1918* (Edinburgh: Polygon, 2015), p. 18.

32. Dorothy McMillan and Michael Byrne (ed.), *Modern Scottish Women Poets* (Canongate: Edinburgh, 2003), p. xii.

33. Norman Harper, Filming on The Cabrach, http://www.stronach.co.uk/2014-02-19/filming-on-the-cabrach.

34. Ian Olsen notes that '…while she was more than willing to contribute to patriotic fund-raising publications during the Great War of 1914-18, she saw all too clearly the way it was leading to hellish destruction of the country's young men, and in February 1916… she published… perhaps the most searing account ever made of that terrible war – *The Glen's Muster-Roll.*' Ian Olsen, 'The College and the Poet' (part 2), *Pelican*, issue 15 (2012).

35. J D McClure, "Lallans' and 'Doric' in North-eastern Scottish Poetry' in *English World-Wide*, 8, 2 (1987, 215-234, p. 43.

36 Trevor Royle (ed.), *In Flanders Field: Scottish Poetry and Prose of the First World War* (Edinburgh: Mainstream: Edinburgh, 1990), p. 21. Also, 'Mary Symon's poetry was a poetry of understanding and sympathy, neither jingoistic or over sentimental. The sheer awfulness and horror is brought home to one community – and by so doing is representative of the pain of so many, many communities across Scotland. That Mary Symon's mother came from the Cabrach, with all the sufferings that it endured during the war years, gives the poem an added poignancy, strength and resonance that can still be experienced today.' [http://www.edinburghswar.ed.ac.uk/sites/default/files/pdf_Mary_Symon_life_and_work_1.pdf].

37. Leslie Wheeler (ed.) *Ten Northeast Poets* (Aberdeen University Press: Aberdeen, 1985), p. 135.

38. See Michael Grieve and Alexander Scott (ed.) *The Hugh MacDiarmid Anthology* (Routledge & Kegan Paul: London, 1972), p. 15:

I met ayont the cairney

A lass wi tousie hair

Singin till a bairnie

That was nae langer there.

Wunds wi' warlds to swing

Dinna sing sae sweet,

The licht that bends owre aa thing

Is less ta'en up wi' it.

Note that MacDiarmid's poem has a folk source, taking some lines from a folk song provided by Allan Ramsay for the *Scots Musical Museum*.

I met ayont the kairney,

Jenny Nettles, Jenny Nettles,

Singing till her bairny,

Robin Rattle's bastard.

39. Judith Kazantis, in the preface to Catherine W Reilly, *Scars Upon My Heart: Women's Poetry and Verse of the First World War* (Virago: London, 1981), p. xvi. See also Deborah Tyler-Bennett, 'Lives Mocked at by Chance: Contradictory Impulses in Women's Poetry of the Great War' in Patrick J Quinn & Steven Trout (ed.) *The Litereature of the Great War Reconsidered* (Palgrave: London, 2001), pp 67-76 and Margaret R Higonnet, 'Women's Poetry of the First World War' in Patrick J Quinn & Steven Trout (ed.) *The Litereature of the Great War Reconsidered* (Palgrave: London, 2001), pp 185-197.

40. James N Alison (ed.) *Poetry of North-east Scotland* (Heinemann: London, 1976), p. 302.

41. This poem was written apparently for *The Graphic* but never published. It is published here for the first time by permission of the Imperial War Museum.

42. 'Millions of wound dressings made from Sphagnum, or 'bog moss', were used during World War I (1914-1918). Dried Sphagnum can absorb up to twenty times its own volume of liquids, such as blood, pus, or antiseptic solution, and promotes antisepsis. Sphagnum was thus superior to inert cotton wool dressings (pure cellulose), the raw material for which was expensive and increasingly being commandeered for the manufacture of explosives. Charles Walker Cathcart, an Edinburgh surgeon, organised collections of the moss throughout Scotland, and centres for its cleaning and preparation. Most collecting was done by women and children (often boy scouts or girl guides) working for long hours in cold, wet bogs.' Peter Ayres, 'Wound Dressing in World War I – The kindly Sphagnum Moss, an unsung hero?' *Field Bryology*, no 110 (2013), 27-34, p. 27.

43. Some of her poems were published as pamphlets in her lifetime. *Wir Roup* can be found in the School of Scottish Studies library of Edinburgh University (F3(4125)) and *The Exile* in the Mitchell Library, Glasgow (821.912).

43. Acc 3501 5.

44. Mary Symon, *Deveron Days* (Aberdeen, D Wylie & Son, 1933).

45. Acc 7534 2.

46. 'In the year of her first poetic triumph, 1933, it is not surprising that Gordon's College turned to her. The highly active 'good works' triumvirate of Dr Walter A Reid, Chairman of the College Governors, John D. Munro, solicitor, and William Tawse, builder, all friends of Mary Symon, invited her to provide the words for a School Song to be incorporated the following year into the Founder's Day play. Founder's Day on the 27th April 1934, was to be a great success, with Baillie John D Munro, Convener of the School Committee, giving a moving account in the morning in the Mither Kirk of the history of the College, together with a remembrance of Robert Gordon. This was attended by the Lord Provost and Magistrates, the College Governors, representatives of the University of Aberdeen and many other public bodies. Wreaths were laid in Drum's Aisle, below the Founder's Memorial Table. The then Headmaster, Graham Andrew, records in The Book of the First Founder's Day: 1934, that 'We are indebted to Miss Mary Symon for the words of the song at the end of Scene V, in Part II.' 'They are able because they perceive they are able' comes from Virgil's *Aeneid*. This was later changed to 'Omni nunc arte magistra – endowed with all that makes for mastery', also from the *Aeneid*, which became the College motto… The play had the Scots title of *The Auld Hoose*. This was the familiar name of the original College building, and indeed, on special occasions previously, Lady Nairne's song, *The Auld Hoose*, had been the music played. Virtually all the play itself was to be in Scots as well, and this would have presented no problem for the actors, for it was the language of the pupils (and probably most of the staff) at the time.' Ian Olsen, 'The College and the Poet' (part 2), *Pelican*, issue 15 (2012).

47. Acc 3501 5.

48. Acc 7534 2.

49. Often her prose writing is over-laden and tautological. For example: ' …trivialities count—everyone who writes knows that—and time and time again the penny candle of the casual philistone has been know to illuminate ever a master's way through the majestic morass of their own words.' (Acc 7534 2). Or this: "But batheration if ye like it', yelled the highland drover to the physiologist who was explaining scientifically why beer should not be drunk… 'If we like it!' It is the 'Siste Viator' in the ear of every reformer, the Ultima Thule in all argument.' from Malcolm Forbes,'Women and Fiction', in *The New Century Review*, Vol. 7 (January-June, 1900), 345-349, 349. Malcolm Forbes was an occasional pen name for Symon.

50. Row warm yir jetties, bonnie dear,

An' aw fir linen claidle
The sweetest tune to Granny's ear,
Is music fae the cradle.
He's sleepin' noo, the canty chiel
Guid bless the bonny laddie,
Ae couthy kiss will Granny steal,
Lors, Sir, he's like his daddie!
Hush-ye-ba, sleep awa:
Dinna wauken mammie
Yir daddie's oot tae catch a troot,
To my bonnie lammie.
Fin ye gang up Deeside a tour,
Wi' mam and dad and Mary,
Ye'll get yir Grannie's Koh-i-noor,
To grace yir new Glengarry
The siller's scarce, yir daddie says,
Shame tak' the British nation,
But I'll gar Willie Gladstone raise,
A million mair taxation.
I'll speak to Paw, aul-farrant sage!
He'll raise the win', I'se warrant,
Though I should sell or e'en mortgage,
Green… to the Baron.
The whiskey is ower dear by far,
I'll gar them mak' it cheaper,
Yir Granny likes her Lochnagar,
Tooth froth? Ay, as weel's her nieper.

(The ellipsis in the fifth last line is due to an obscurity in the manuscript).

WAR
POEMS

The Soldiers' Cairn

GIE me a hill wi' the heather on't,
  An' a reid sun drappin' doon,
Or the mists o' the mornin' risin' saft
    Wi' the reek owre a wee grey toon.
Gie me a howe by the lang Glen road,
    For it's there 'mang the whin an' fern
(D'ye mind on't, Will? Are ye hearin', Dod?)
    That we're biggin' the Soldiers' Cairn.

Far awa' is the Flanders land
    Wi' fremmit France atween,
But mony a howe o' them baith the day
    Has a hap o' the Gordon green;
It's them we kent that's lyin' there,
    An' it's nae wi' stane or airn,
But wi' brakin' herts, an' mem'ries sair
    That we're biggin' the Soldiers' Cairn.

Doon, laich doon the Dullan sings—
    An' I ken o' an aul' sauch tree,
Where a wee loon's wahnie's hingin' yet
    That's dead in Picardy;
An' ilka win' fae the Conval's broo
    Bends aye the buss o' ern,
Where aince he futtled a name that noo
    I'll read on the Soldiers' Cairn.

Oh! build it fine an' build it fair,

Till it leaps to the moorland sky—
More, more than death is symbolled there,
    Than tears or triumphs by.
There's the Dream Divine of a starward way
    Oor laggard feet would learn—
It's a new earth's corner-stone we'd lay
    As we fashion the Soldiers' Cairn.

Lads in your plaidies lyin' still,
    In lands we'll never see,
This lanely cairn on a hameland hill
    Is a' that oor love can dee;
An' fine an' braw we'll mak' it a',
    But oh, my Bairn, my Bairn,
It's a cradle's croon that'll aye blaw doon
    To me fae the Soldiers' Cairn.

The Glen's Muster-Roll

The Dominie Loquitur:

HING 't up aside the chumley-cheek, the aul' glen's
　　Muster Roll,
A' names we ken fae hut an' ha', fae Penang to the Pole,
An' speir na gin I'm prood o't—losh! coont them
　　line by line,
Near han' a hunner fechtin' men, an' they a' were
　　Loons o' Mine.

A' mine. It's jist like yesterday they sat there raw on raw,
Some tyaavin' wi' the' Rule o' Three,' some widin'
　　throu' 'Mensa';
The map o' Asia's shoogly yet faur Dysie's sheemach head
Gaed cleeter-clatter a' the time the carritches was said.
'A limb', his greetin' granny swore, 'the aul' deil's
　　very limb'—
But Dysie's deid and drooned lang syne; the Cressy
　　coffined him.
'Man guns upon the fore barbette!' …What's that
　　to me an' you?
Here's moss an' burn, the skailin' kirk, aul' Kissack
　　beddin's soo.
It's Peace, it's Hame—but owre the Ben the coastal
　　searchlights shine,
And we ken that Britain's bastions mean—that sailor
　　Loon o' Mine.

The muirlan's lang, the muirlan's wide, an' fa says
　　'ships' or 'sea'?

But the tang o saut that's in wir bleed has puzzled mair
   than me.
There's Sandy wi' the bristled shins, faur think ye's he
   the day?
Oot where the hawser's tuggin' taut in the surf o' Suvla Bay;
An' owre the spurs o' Chanak Bahr gaed twa lang
   stilpert chiels,
I think o' flappin' butteries yet or weyvin' powets' creels—
Exiles on far Australian plains—but the Lord's ain
   boomerang
'S the Highland heart that's aye for hame hooever far
   it gang.
An' the winds that wail owre Anzac an' requiem Lone Pine
Are nae jist a' for stranger kin, for some were
   Loons o' Mine.

They're comin' hame in twas an' threes; there's Tam
   fae Singapore—
Yon's his, the string o' buckie-beads abeen the aumry door—
An' Dick Macleod, his sanshach sel' (Guidsake, a bombardier!)
I see them yet ae summer day come hodgin' but the fleer:
'Please, sir' (a habber an' a hoast), 'Please, sir' (a gasp, a gulp,
Syne wi' a rush) 'Please—sir—can—we—win—oot—
   to—droon—a—fulp?'
…Hi, Rover, here, lad!—ay, that's him, the fulp they
   didna droon,
But Tam—puir Tam lies cauld an' stiff on some grey Belgian dune,
An' the *Via Dolorosa*'s there, faur a wee bit cutty quine
Stan's lookin' doon a teem hill road for a sodger
   Loon o' Mine.

Fa's neist? The Gaup—A Gordon wi' the 'Bydand' on
   his broo,

Nae murlacks dreetlin' fae his pooch or owre his grauvit noo,
Nae word o' groff-write trackies on the 'Four best ways
    to fooge'—
He steed his grun' an' something mair, they tell me,
    oot at Hooge.
But owre the dyke I'm hearin' yet: 'Lads, fa's on for
    a swap?—
A lang sook o' a pandrop for the sense o' *verbum sap.*
Fack's death, I tried to min' on 't—here's my gairten wi'
    the knot—
But—bizz! a dhubrack loupit as I passed the muckle pot.'
…Ay, ye didna ken the classics, never heard o' a co-sine,
But here's my aul'lum aff' tae ye, dear gowkit
    Loon o' Mine.

They're handin' oot the haloes, an' three's come to
    the glen—
There's Jeemack ta'en his Sam Browne to his mither's
    but an' ben.
Ay, they ca' me 'Blawin' Beelie,' but I never crawed
    sae crouse
As the day they gaed the VC to my *filius nullius.*
But he winna sit 'Receptions' nor keep on his aureole,
A' he says is 'Dinna haiver, jist rax owre the Bogie Roll.' An'
the Duke an' 's dother shook his han' an' speirt aboot
    his kin.
'Old family, yes; here sin' the Flood,' I smairtly chippit in.
(Fiech! Noah's? Na—we'd ane wirsels, ye ken, in '29.) I'm
nae the man tae stan' an' hear them lichtlie
    Loon o' Mine.
Wir Lairdie. That's his mither in her doo's-neck silk gaun by,

The podduck, so she tells me, 's haudin' up the H.L.I.
An' he's stan'in' owre his middle in the Flanders'
    clort an' dub,
Him 'at eese't to scent his hanky, an' speak o's mornin' 'tub.'
The Manse loon's dellin' divots on the weary road to Lille,
An' he canna flype his stockin's, cause they hinna
    tae nor heel.
Sennelager's gotten Davie—a' moo fae lug tae lug—
An' the Kaiser's kyaak, he's writin', 'll neither ryve nor rug,
'But mind ye' (so he post-cairds), 'I'm already owre
    the Rhine.'
Ay, there's nae a wan worth o' them, though they werena
    Loons o' Mine.

…You—Robbie. Memory pictures: Front bench,
    a curly pow,
A chappit hannie grippin' ticht a Homer men't wi' tow—
The lave a' scrammelin' near him, like bummies roon a bike.
'Fat's this?' 'Fat's that?'. He'd tell them a'—ay,
    speir they fat they like.
My hill-foot lad! A' sowl an' brain fae's bonnet to his
    beets.
A 'Fullarton' *in posse*, nae the first fun' fowin' peats.
…An' I see a blythe young Bajan gang whistlin' doon
    the brae,
An' I hear a wistful Paladin his patriot credo say.
An' noo, an' noo I'm waitin' till a puir thing hirples hame—
Ay, 't's the Valley o' the Shadow, nae the mountain
    heichts o' Fame.
An' where's the nimble nostrum, the dogma fair and fine,
To still the ruggin' heart I hae for you, oh,
    Loon o' Mine?

My Loons, my Loons! Yon winnock gets the settin' sun
the same,
Here's sklates and skailies, ilka dask a' futtled wi' a name.
An' as I sit a vision comes: Ye're troopin' in aince mair,
Ye're back fae Aisne an' Marne an' Meuse, Ypres an'
Festubert;
Ye're back on weary bleedin' feet—you, you that danced
an' ran—
For every lauchin' loon I kent I see a hell-scarred man.
Not mine but yours to question now! You lift unhappy
eyes—
'Ah, Maister, tell's fat a' this means.' And I, ye thocht
sae wise,
Maun answer wi' the bairn words ye said tae me langsyne:
'I dinna ken, I dinna ken. Fa does, oh, Loons o' Mine?'

A Recruit for the Gordons

I'M aff! The halflin gets my crib,
An' keeps the chaumer key;
 The morn aul' Mains can dicht his nib,
  An' scoor the lift for me.

 I've listed! Dang the nowt an' neeps!
  I'm aff' to fecht or fa';
I ken, withoot their weary threeps,
They're mair than needin's a'.

Wi' Huns upon wir thrashel-stane,
 An' half the world red wud,
Gweed sax feet ane o' brawn an' bane
 Is nae for plooman dud.

An' sae I paumered back an' fore,
 Practeesin' in my kilt,
An' Sownock fae the bothy door
 Kame-sowfed a martial lilt.

They leuch till howe an' hill-tap rang—
 I steppit safe mysel'—
For aye anaith my bonnet sang
 Bit things I couldna tell—

The bonnet wi' the aul' 'Bydand'
 That sat upon my broo—
An' something stirred, grey Mitherland,
 In my puir hert for you.

As aye an' aye the plaidie green
   Swung roon my naked knee,
An', mairchin' there anaith the meen,
   Lord sake! That wasna me.

The eat-meat sumph that kissed the quines,
   An' took a skyte at Eel;
I was the heir o' brave langsynes,
   A sodger, head to heel.

Ay me! 'At never shot a craw,
   Nor killed a cushey-doo—
But bleed's aye bleed, an' aul granda
   Did things at Waterloo.

I'm aff the morn…There's nane'll ken
   O' ae broon curly head,
That ees't to lie aside my ain
   In Mains's stoupet bed.

It's laich, laich noo, in Flanders sod,
   An' I'm mairchin' wi' the drum,
'Cause doon the lang La Bassée road
   There's dead lips cryin' 'Come!'

After Neuve Chapelle

WE'D a hefty second horseman fae the braes on
     Deveronside,
An' twa bit College birkies like to burst their breeks
     wi' pride;
There was Lauchin' Tam an' 'Curly' an' the ane we
     ca'ed 'the Loon',
Wi' his sowf an' pech an' fosel, fit to wreck the hale platoon.
An' they're a' deid or deein'—I've a gey bit clour mysel'—
But I winner fat they're thinkin' i' the Glen, o'
     Neuve Chapelle.

Man, I wish I'd seen the smiddy the nicht the news
     cam in!
The Bailie's beld head noddin', the Soutar clawin' 's chin,
The country clashes fleein' as the sun gied doon the Lecht,
Till the paper geat comes skirlin': 'The Gordons in a
     Fecht.'
Losh! I think I see them loupin'—'Gi' es 't!' 'Heely,
     man, 't'll tear!'
'Faur are they?' 'Read it!' 'Fat is 't?' An' the Bailie
     smores a swear
As he hicks an' mants: 'H'm! Fiech—It's wait—I'll need
     to spell'—
(It's a geylies chancy mou'fu' that Frenchy Neuve Chapelle).

Syne they'll read about La Bassée an' the red roofs o' Aubers,
An' like kitlins in the kinkhost they'll try Armentières;
An' the Smith'll rax his weskit fae the nail upo' the wa'—
'I'm dootin' that's Will Lowry's lot; I'll gi'e the wife a ca.'

Puir Will! to lye oor Hielan' strath for (Lord!) a Street
   o' Hell,
I'll nae gi'e Jinse his full address, I'll jist say
   New Shapelle.'

O sair o' heart they'll be, I ken 't'll pit them aff
   their brose,
An' the Bellman'll be dichtin' mair than sneeshan-draps
   fae's nose,
As the pumphels fill on Sunday, an' aside the pulpit stair
They'll see the Roll o' Honour, an' the names o'
   deid men there.
But the Parson winna haiver; I can hear the rafters ring:
'They have garnered earth's best glory, who have died for
   Home and King.'
(He's the deil to spout, oor billie!) It's a slogan, nae a knell,
That'll soun' in grey Kiltairlie owre the graves at
   Neuve Chapelle.

A slogan! Ay, they're needn't. Gang doon the Glen
   at nicht :
There's twa lang loons o' Muirton's at the fireside warm
   an' ticht.
There's Boggies snarin' myaukens, an' his neiper
   buskin' flees,
An' the Mason's at the dambrod for the Belgian refugees.
They're dancin', singin', fiddlin', an' owre a rim o' sea
We're treadin'—ay, we're treadin'—each man a Calvary.
Oh, glens that gave the Gordons, is't you will give as well
The cohorts of the damned and done that heed nae
   Neuve Chapelle?

God! Will they ever wauken, the loons that sit at hame?
While din-faced Sikhs an' Ghurkas fecht to keep oor
    shores fae shame.
Oor kin fae a' the Seven Seas are tummelin' to the fray,
But there's laggards yet on lown hillsides 'neath skies that
    span the Spey,
On braes where Charlie's banner flew, an' Jean sae
    kindly kissed,
Where the very peweet's yammer is a wistfu' 'Loon
    gang 'list'—
Man, I canna thole the thocht o't. But when this cursed
    welter's deen,
I widna like to be the man that stan's in slacker's sheen.
My bairns'll never blush for me; my teem
    sark-sleeve'll tell
I did my bit for hame an' them ae day at
    Neuve Chapelle

For Our Empire

MEN of our Race! You great of old,
   Across the stretching years,
Give of your fires to hearts grown cold,
   Speak Faith in faithless ears;
Your dead hands to their task again—
   Flash high the beacon red,
To gather men. They must be men
   That sires like you have bred.

Men of our Race! You, you that trod
   Our glens but yesterday,
What if you sleep in Flanders sad,
   Or far by Suvla Bay?
You're speaking yet; your wistful eyes
   Seek still yon strip of foam,
To bid our laggard legions rise
   And strike today for home!

Men of our Race! The stars grow dim
   Above our island sea;
No paeans now: the battle hymn
   Sinks to a threnody.
'Tis Britain's hour! She hears the tread
   Of feet that pass her by';
Behind the ramparts of her dead
   She sees the Beast draw nigh.
'Tis Britain's hour! Which will it be?—
   Her nadir or her noon?

We look in your young eyes and see,
　O Loon, O Sodger Loon!

A Whiff o' Hame

(Written as an introduction to a Christmas book
sent to the fighting men in 1916)

A HANSEL! Lads in khaki,
  An' you in sailor's blue—
But this time it isn't baccy,
    'Woodbines' or 'Honeydew'.
It's neither grub nor grauvat,
    It's neither sark nor sock,
It's nae the Psalms o' Dauvit,
    Nor 'Stop yer ticklin', Jock.'

It's—weesht'—A norland river
    Gaun soochin' to the sea;
It's the mists abeen Loch Lomond,
    An' the stars owre Benachie.
It's a lovelilt fae a gloarnin',
    When' a' the world was kind!
It's a step gaun up the loanin'
    O' frien's you left behind;
It's a hand-clasp fae your kindred,
    It's a word fae hearts aflame
Wi' love an' pride o' you, lads—
    Ay-it's jist a whiff o' Hame.

You're back the surf at Saros,
    Where the cloud-wrack hides the moon,
You're fittin't 'mong the Pharaohs,
    Or bombin' at Bethune;

You're in weary fremmit places
   That oor tongues can hardly name—
But it's couthy fires, kent faces,
   Wi' this wee whiff o' Hame.

Oor Hame! Ah, lad, oot yonder!
   Fa dreams o' suns that shone
On Britain's young-day splendour,
   On glories past and gone?
The eyes are surely holden,
   Dull, dead, that canna see
That the day that's great and golden
   Is the day that gave us Thee—
To stand by trench and halyard,
   To ache, an' fecht, an' fa',
As ye cry: 'The old Land's worth it—
   Dear God, it's worth it a!'

Bill Smith's Chum Says

WHAT d'ye think we're doin',
      Mam and the girls and me'
Sittin' down in the drill hall,
All busy as busy can be?
And the old chap round the corner,
And the boy that wants a leg,
And the big brown gent from India,
What talks o' 'havin' a peg',
And the ladies up from the Grand Hotel,
All covered wi' diamond rings,
And the little white-faced orphan,
that stands in the street and sings:
Now what d'ye think we're doin'?
Prayer-meeting? Pitch an' toss?
Ah well, ye'd better give it up, for ye'd *never* guess,
Why, we're all of us pickin' moss.

Moss from the silent moorland,
Moss from the green braeside—
And it's goin' away in the troopships,
That sail wi' the windy tide:
It's goin' to France and Belgium,
To the Ancre and the Somme—
Some of it's goin' to Egypt,
Maybe some of it bidin' at home:
But all of it's goin' to someone—
(My, don't the thing sound queer?)
To someone who's shedding his blood for us,

All sittin' so cosy here,
Our moss wi' the sun upon it,
And highland rain and dew,
Growin' in God's own garden,
Dear soldier lads, for you.

Pickin' moss for the soldiers!
It's the finest ploy we have!
It's jest all Hist'ry pipin' hot,
'Bout Teuton, Gaul and Slav—
It's the war lookin' in at the window,
And the whizz-bangs goin' by,
And our khakis standin' row on row,
'Neath the blue of a far-off sky,
Or maybe tis the dusk that's fallin',
Wi' our khakis lyin' still,
Face down—in the clay—as they told us,
On the crest of Hulluch Hill,
…Well, that's that's where the moss is goin',
And you'd like it if you knew,
What queer things go with it,
Oh, soldier lads, to you.

There's Betty, look, in the corner,
She sits and wipes her eyes,
And once we would ha' laughed at her,
Wi' her snuffly sobs and sighs:
But we don't laugh now worth mentionin',
My chum, Bill Smith an' me,
'Cause we think of the boy as she lost last year,
Away in the cold North Sea.

… Oh, yes, It's the moss we're doin',
But, by gum, the moss ain't all.
There's a mighty lot o' thinkin'
Been done in this 'ere hall.
Why, folks as were hardly speakin'
An' hating each other like mad,
Jest over the moor has been lovin' and kind,
As they think o' some soldier lad
Who's fightin' away out yonder,
Fightin' for Earth's Big Things
An' makin' them sick ashamed o' sulks
An' swappin' digs an' flings.
…Ay, I think we're growing better,
Kinder and straighter too,
An' it's all along o' the moss, you know,
An' soldier lads o' you.

LOCAL VERNACULAR POEMS

The Wag-At-The-Wa'

A UL' sconface we ca'ed it, hairst-bap an' the like—
A' pictered wi' hoosies, an' bees, an' a bike,
Wi' dosses o' roses meanderin' roon—
Oh! a plenishin' gran', baith for sicht an' for soun'—
The but-the-hoose cheeper had muntins nae mous,
The lever could tell's fan tae yoke an' tae lowse,
O' the aul' kitchey caser we couldna weel blaw,
But losh! we wis prood o' oor Wag-at-the-wa',

It briested ye straucht as ye opened the door;
Maybe ae 'oor ahin, maybe twa-three afore.
'Bit fiech! Fat o' that?' the aul' man would say,
'A college curriculum's oor time o' day!'
An' tappin' his mullie, he'd stot awa' ben,
'Noo, ye see, lads, the han's at the hauf aifter ten,
An' it's new chappit ane—Weel, Greenwich an' me
Positeevely can state—*it's a quarter fae three!*
Ay! Logic, Algebra—ye sair nott them a'
When ye set oat to bothom oor Wag-at-the-wa''.'

The fun that we made o't! The lauchs that we got!
I could tell them a' yet, though the greet's in my throat.
...Aul' chap, on yir kopje (or is't a karoo?),
Div ye min' the Eel-even, when some ane got fou?
When the reel 'naith the rafters was ill for his queet,
But he'd dance, he could swear, the backstep on a peat;
When wi' little persuasion he sang to the cat,
An' tellt the stuffed oolet jist a' fat was fat;

But to ken foo't a' ended, an' fa' bested fa—
Weel, I'd need to *sub pœna* the Wag-at-the-wa'.

An' Jean, ye're awa' amon' bleckies to bide!
Ye're rich an' ye're gran', an' 'my lady' beside;
But fyles, wi' yir fine things an' fair things a' roon,
Will yer een maybe fill, an' yir heart gie a stoon?
As the aul' days come back; the lad at the door,
An' the 'weeshtin', till owre the stair-head comes a snore.
Syne, oh! lassie, syne—but I winna say mair—
A' the glamour an' glory o' life met ye there,
An' Heaven cam' gey near to the wearyfu' twa
That kissed their first kiss 'naith the Wag-at-the-wa'.

Ay, we're a' scattered noo, but it's aye tickin' on—
Ye hear't at the dykeside, ye hear't up the loan—
Ye hear't—divn't ye, lad? by the lang lippin' seas
That soom by yir doorcheek at the Antipodes.
An' Tam, wi' yir tackets on Ottawa's steep,
What is't that comes hack when ye canna get sleep?
Jist the croon o' a burn in a far-awa' glen,
The clink o' a churn, or a fit comin' ben,
An' in laich obligato, the lift an' the fa',
The sab an' the sang o' a Wag-at-the-wa'.

Day's aifter ilk dawnin' an' nicht aifter e'en;
But there's nae steppin' back owre the gait we ha'e gane;
An' Fate winna huckster, or tell fat she'd ha'e
To lan' me a loon again, doon the aul' brae—
Wi' the lang road afore: wad I bide? wad I gang?
Ah, me! I ken noo, but the kennin's ta'en lang .
…Though kind's been the farin', an' crownèd the quest,

For the bit that's gane by me, I'd swap a' the rest.
The braw beild is yonder I set oot tae win,
An' Ichabod's up or the door I'm weel in.
There was sun on the summit I ettled to speel,
But it's mirk noo I'm up, an' I'm weary as weel
What's glory? What's gold? A quate heart's worth them a',
An' I left mine langsyne by a Wag-at-the-wa'.

Old and New

IN vino veritas!
That's the classic wye
   O' Horace owre his glass,
      In times lang bye.
A' credit to the lad for his acumen—
         But on ony norland brae,
         Ye can hear the same the day,
         Faur we jist mak oot to say,
'A foo man's a true man.'

Fan the halflin' coups his gill,
   (An' fat for no?)
An' the lordy's had a swill
   O' Veuve Cliquot,
They're baith sic-like—the plutocrat an' plooman,
      For the craitur 'naith the clout,
      Has a wye o' keekin' oot,
      An' ye'll nae be lang in doobt,
That a foo man's a true man.

Aye the brimmin' quaich!
   Aye the bonnie quine!
The love-lilt, sweet an' laich—
   The threesome divine!
Lat's hae them a' be't penny trump or Schumann—
      But lat's mislippen nane—
      When we pree the tappit hen,
      Fat's but'll aye come ben,
For a foo man's a true man.

Here's lookin' to ye, Horace!
    When Virgil supped wi' you—
An' owre your doch-an-doris,
    The twa o' ye got fou—
Had ye to thole, like's a', the tongue o' woman?
        For in far awa' B.C.
        I misdoot if Lalagé
        'Dulce loquens' aye wad be
Owre the foo man an' the true man.

The Aucht Day Clock

WE'VE flitted, lad, we've flitted,
　　We've left the aul' close mou';
We're tryin' to be gentry,
　　Wi' oor gilt an' ormolu.
The hoose is fu' o' bravities,
　　An' a' new-fangled trock,
But I'd swap them a' the morn
　　For my guid auld aucht-day clock.

I mind on't in the hoose at hame,
　　My granny's but-an-ben ;
Her owre-croon mutch aside it sat,
　　Her specs an' sneeshan pen;
An' throu' the wee gell winnock aye
　　Fu' bonnie mornin' broke,
As I binnered back the bed door
　　To see what 'twas o'clock.

The aumry wi' the cheena cups,
　　A' spreckled reid an' blue,
The soord that Uncle Willie took
　　Bleed-red fae Waterloo—
Were gran' eneuch: the kist o' drawers
　　Was nae a' thing to mock;
But ane an' a', they bouket sma'
　　Aside the aucht-day clock.

Its canny jow gied throu' the hoose
　　Like some laich-chanted spell.

It cried, 'Ye jaud, ye fuged the school,'
　　It speired, 'Fa bosied Bell?'
It grat abeen the coffin-lid,
　　It timed the cradle's rock,
An' the lilts that rang in Eden
　　Cam' fae the aucht-day clock.

I'm missin't, losh, I'm missin't,
　　The shielin's gane langsyne;
The braes where eence I wandered
　　Nae mair ken tread o' mine.
A far-aff win' blaws owre them,
　　I'm my lane 'mong fremmit folk,
Since my hinmost frien' has left me,
　　My guid auld aucht-day clock.

Burns Nicht in the Glen
(by the chairman, Jock o' Durns)

My blacks! Lay oot my Sunday blacks,
  Upo' the chaumer bed:
Syne steek the door, an' tell the fowk
  I'm drunk, or daft, or dead.
There's things byordnar' on the nicht—
  Redd up the horn-en',
An' set the duck'shner to my han'
  Wi' paper, ink, and pen.
An' nae ae cheep; nae rants nor rows,
  Nae clyte o' cogs or churns;
In lanely maijesty I'm aff
  To mak' a speech on Burns.

Aweel, I'm but. I powk the peats,
  An' draw my chair inbye:
I gaur, I glow'r, an' scrat my head,
  An' pech an' say 'Ay, ay.'
Noo for a stairt, There's 'Gentlemen',
  Reeled aff as swack's ye like—
Fair copperplate—but—fat's that din?
  Confound that yelpin' tyke!
An' someane's bowffin' 'Bonnie Doon'
  Gaun by my very gell!
Lash fa could stan' a strain like this
  On tea an' traickle ale?
My back's a stripe, my mou's a kiln;
  I'm het an' caul' by turns,

But never mind. Rin dog, rin deil,
　　I'll mak' that speech on Burns.

Weel, syne I rise an' rax my shins,
　　An' sclaffer owre the fleer;
Aye thinkin' fat's been said o' him
　　For many a lang, lang year.
There's them that ca's him seer an' sage,
　　There's them that ca's him king;
There's preans piped wad gar ye greet,
　　An' them that mak' ye sing.
Ah me!
　　　　　But weesht!
　　　　　　　Is't dwawm or dream?
　　Yon whispered: 'Jock o' Durns,
There's naething left anaith the lift
　　By noo to say o' Burns.'

I ken't. There's naething. Nae ae wird;
It's a' been said lang syne—
Dazed, ooled, I stoiter to the door
　　An' watch the starnies shine,
Owre muir an' moss, owre hill an' howe,
　　Owre a' the reekin' lums,
Till fae the glen's still heart to mine
　　Swift, sweet, a solace comes,
All' dirlin' through my auld grey pow,
　　My dool to gledness turns,
For noo I ken there's something yet
　　We a' can dee for Burns.

It's this: To keep the wealth he gae's,

The tongue that's a' oor ain.
Fat though a witless world misca's—
   Oh, owre an' owre again—
Let's tryst upon oor lea-rigs yet,
   Let's speed oor banks an' braes,
An', till the farthest sun has set,
   Sing on oor 'Scots wha hae's'.
Let's ne'er forget 'A Man's a Man'
   Thrills earth fae sea to sea—
The Magna Charta Scotland gave
   To a' humanity.
Oh, puir's his soul, an' caul's his bleed,
   The patriot prayer that spurns:
'Lord keep the heather on oor hills,
   An' in oor hearts oor Burns!'

Oh, English speech for English yird!
   We ken it's grand an' fine:
But ah! it tak's the dear Scots word
   To grip your heart an' mine.
Ill-faured, an' rude, an' roch it's ca'ed,
   Wanworth an' a' the rest;
But—hands across the heather, lad—
   We ken oor ain kens best.
We ken the faiths, the dreams it's nursed
   On ilka hill an' glen;
We ken what mak's the Scot the first
   'Mong a' the breed o' men.
We ken—an't needs nae fykes o' phrase,
   Nae screeds on 'storied urns'—
Oor best we got fae misty braes,
   Oor mither tongue, an' Burns.

We've gowd upon oor Lammas rigs,
  We've gowd upon oor whin,
But, ah, the gowd that's worth them a'—
  Cam' wi' a Jan'war win'.
An' aye that win'—it's blawin' yet—
Gang doon an Alford brae:
An'—bonnets aff, lads, bonnets aff—
  To hear yon 'Whistle' play.
Oh, Robin's chair for lang's been teem,
  Lat Charlie tak' it noo—
An' twine the heather an' the breem—
  A laurel for his broo.
He's gien's 'The Packman's' pawky blaw,
  He's gien's yon fair 'Green Yule,'
He's gien's the loonie, sib till's a',
  Gaun doiterin' to the school—
He's gien's the joy the laverock lilts,
  The wae the pee-weet mourns,
He's ta'en us back, he's ta'en us back
  The lang road hame to Burns.

The Wedding
(by an Opposite Neighbour)

SEE, here's the bridegroom, Kirsty,
　I ken him by his breeks,
　　His chumley-hat and dickey,
　　　An' the way he bobs an' keeks
　　Like a hen that's heark'nin' thunner,
　　　Or a corbie seekin' 's hole,
　　He'll be mirkier at his burial
　　　Tho' he winna look as droll.

　　I winner gin they're ready noo;
　　　There's reek in ilka lum,
　　An' there's the aul' vricht, he's been in
　　　To set the table plumb.
　　Wheest! There's the quarter chappin',
　　　They'll be a' here in a breist;
　　Is that the pock-faced lawyer
　　　An' his mither? Ay, it's jist.

Humph! Some ane spak' o' gentry
　　Guid save's gin they be a'—
Him stinkit up wi' hair-ile
　　That ye'd smell a mile awa',
An' her—a nochty craiter,
　　Choke-fu' o' fulsome wile—
But—ay, that's Willie Muncy,
　　I thocht I kent the tile;

An' that's his father's weskit,

I'll bet ye half-a-croon;
I min' his mither tellin' me
   She thocht o' makin' 't doon,
An' there's the lassie Taylor—
   Losh! Foo they're steerin' in,
They hinna missed a livin' sowl
   Fae Badenoch to the Binn,

Fat wis't the wifie said yestreen
   When spreadin' oot the braws?
I kent she'd something in her crap,
   Wi' a' her hums an' haws;
That Annie's lad had cheated you!
   She hadna't hardly oot
Afore I had her fire's her mutch,
   An' mim's a chokit troot.

I tell you I was in a pirr,
   'Yon peesweep!' Syne I leugh,
An' then she speired me gin I thocht
   Ae kebbuck was eneugh.
It's growin' dark, come lass, an' edge
   My chair a thochtie ben,
An' lift the screen—But fat's that noo,
   Anither rosten hen?

That mak's a score.
   I wish I had the feathers an' the banes;
But loshy, there's the bride an' groom
   Jist jinkin' aff their lanes.
An' save us! foo he's kissin' her!
   Hoots! dinna licht the licht,
It's mony a day sin' I hae seen

Half sic a humblin' sicht.
Oh, kiss awa', ere sax month's gane

Ye'll baith be tired o' that!
Faur are ye, Kirsty? Mercy on's,
    That wasna you that grat?
It wasna. Well, you're unco short,
    Ye'll better mask the tay;
Ay, there's the bride an' groom; they'll get
    The meen gaun owre the brae.

Wir Roup
(30th January, 1918)

IT's a', it's a' for the Sodger Lads,
 That in wir he'rts we name;
They're hungry, weary, caul' an' weet,
 While we sit saft at hame,
An' yer hin'maist plack—it's fa wad hain?
 Or yer hin'maist bit an' houp?
So tak' yer ways up the Sergeant's Lane,
 An' help wi' the Sodgers' Roup.

Wir Roup! Ay haith, that wis a Roup!
 They cam' fae Spey an' A'an;
They breisted bogs, they 'rastled owre
 Sic raiths as ne'er wis blawn.
They cam' wi' stirks, they cam' wi' strae,
 They cam' wi' horse an' hen;
The road wis black wi' booin' back
 Near hauf-wye up the Glen.
The Cabrach cam'; and Glass, nae blate,
 Gaed pechin' owre Corsemauld;
The Crachie Brig near shook its foun'
 Wi' frauchts fae field an' fauld.
Fae Deveron, Dullan, Fiddichside,
 A' that could wag a fit,
Gaed doon to Laichie's bonnie howe
 To dee their frien'ly bit.

An' sic a menyie! Cairns o' this,

An' cairns o' that, nae mous!
Wi' gigs an' prams an' flauchter-spauds,
　　An' cairts an' heuks an' hyous.
The canty wives laid kebbucks doon,
　　An' scones an' butter-pats,
An' Wasties steed on gaird aside
　　A ruck o' aul' lum hats.
An', losh keeps a', amo' the curn
　　I kent the Saiddler's tile,
The ane he lent, ae byous day,
　　Till's frien', douce Auchnagyle.
Ye min' the story? Foo we leuch!
　　An' foo the aul' man grat!
As aye the cloody climax cam'—
　　'My guid, new, guinea hat!
Nae mair o' len'in' lums for me
　　In frien'ship's sacred name!
Like a concertina in a cloot,
　　That's foo my hat cam' hame!' …
An' noo on caird or cadger's pow
　　The aul' lum's like to sit,
But a king wi's croon could dae nae mair
　　Than jist his honest bit.

Oot-bye wis raws o' tattie pyocks,
　　An' neeps an' bows o' meal,
An' in a cannie neukie steed
　　An' antrin cask o' ale.
Aul' Cairnies reemisht in a hearse
　　(Its eese we didna speer,
On caul' meenlichts he reested in't,
　　An' nicket aff the deer).

'A hearse,' says he, ''s a handy thing
   To hae aboot yer toon,
But ca't a sheetin-box gin sae
   Ye better like the soun',
A sheetin'-box for life—an mair—
   For deid, ye needna flit;
Speak up noo, lads, fa's gettin' this
   Is handselled deein's bit.'

Syne there wis leems an' sic-like trok—
   They ca' them noo 'anteeks'—
Wee bowlies, juggies, tea-pots, plates
   Fae hamely dresser cheeks
An' ane a' owre wi' roses red,
   An' rimmed wi' gowden stars,
I min' on't in a wee cot-hoose
   On Kirsty's kist o' drawers.
But that's lang syne, an' Kirsty's deid,
   An' the wee bit hoosie's doon,
An' the juggie's here to help to hap
   Some cauldrife Sodger Loon...
An' sae I mused, till Mains gaun by
   Jist gae my tail a tit,
'The juggie's fa'an to Skinflint Tam,
   An' his bit's a thripenny bit!'
So guid an' gran' the bodes began,
   An' e'er the day was deen,
We thanked the Lord wha'd left's wi' nocht
   But twa mismarrowed sheen.

An' Sodger Lad, when oor wee bit
   Gangs owre the sea to you,

Will ye hear the win' at your ain brae-fit
   An' the burnie soughin' through?
Will ye hear the whaup on the hills again?
   But abeen them a, my dear,
There's a voice o' love fae yer ain fire-en'
   That we'd like ye best to hear.

Lichtlied

BOSIKINS, Bosikins, faur hae ye been ?
Tryin' to tak' glamourie fae a muckit gowk's een
(Ay, it wasna that ye ca'd him, or ye bunged a month yestreen).

Bosikins, tell me, was he mournin' sair for me?
Aweel, it wasna deidly grief, sae far as ane could see,
He'd ae lass reen the middle an' anither on his knee.

Bosikins, Bosikins, fat did ye hear?
Some ane ca'ed a Licht-o' Love, an' me mysel' a leear,
But a' the lave I'm keepin' so ye needna fash to speir.

Bosikins, Bosikins, my heart you'll surely brak!
Weel, I'll souther't for a saxpence, or gie yir siller back,
There's anither wanter waitin' an' I'll pit him on your track.

Bosikins, Bosikins, is't true that love aye tires?
Maybe. But hearken what they sing at shearin's in the shires—
'They've Hell by han' that rake amon' the ashes o' deid fires.'

Oor Doric Dead!

OOR Doric dead! But nay, lads, nay—
    The heather haps the hill;
There's aye the breem upon the brae,
    And living, pulsing, still
The word lilts o' oor hill-foot tongue—
    The bairn, the loon, the quine,
The heuch, the howe, the but, the ben
    That made oor dear langsyne.

Oor Doric dead! We've aiblins yet;
    The gype's aye to the fore;
There's sneeters, footers, shargars, sclypes,
    Gaun stoufin' by the door;
We're gettin' amscachs, dirds an' dunts,
    But aye we tchyave awa;
We've spunk an' smeddum i' oor pows
    To thole lye's ilka thraw.

Oor Doric Dead! Some eeschaw says't!
    I tak' my 'Hamewith' doon,
An' turn wi' severant hand the page
    That maks oor Doric croon—
Rime troke na there. The Deevilock's lauch,
    The Packman on the road,
The Whistle's Song—they'll a' be here
    When we're anaith the clod.

It's ill to girn, it's waur to greet—
    But may the Lord forgive

The puir Cassandra creed that wiles
 Sic wealth fae you and me,
—Speak nae o' harps wi' muted strings,
 O' sangs that hae been sung
Fae hert to lip the aul' prayer springs!
 'Long live our Scottish tongue!'

TRANSLATIONS

The Hedonist
(after Béranger)

I KENT o' a king o' the Cabrach aince,
　　An' a gey bit kingie was he;
He had nae sowl, nae siller, nor sense,
　　But did fine withoot a' three,
For he sleepit, ochone! an' snored, ochone!
　　A' day in his beddie ba'—
Wi' a tosselled trok o' it nicht-kep on,
　　An' his croon in the crap o the wa',
　　　　Ay, his bonnie croon,
　　　　Wi' the roset foun'.
　　　　It lay in the crap o' the wa'.

He'd wauken fyles when the knock wad chap,
　　An' skirl fae the horn en'—
'Ye louts, ye loons, I've an awfu' yapp,
　　Fess plates an' trenchers ben;
An' dinna forget, I've a drooth evenoo
　　That could drink the Deveron dry—
An' the mair o' guid ye pit into my mou',
　　The mair'll come oot, say I,
　　　　Oh, better for you,
　　　　A king hauf-fou',
　　　　A hantle, than ane that's dry.'

Weel suppered an' slockit, they'd saiddle him
　　On a shalt as sweer's himsel',
An' he'd ride his realm fae the Rooster's rim

To the lythe o' the Balloch well;
A' his bodygaird was a fozelin' tyke
   As ready to row's to run—
'I'm a king,' says he, 'I can dae as I like
   An' I'm giein' my fowk their fun—
      'He gar't's a' laugh,'
      Is the epitaph,
      I wad like when I'm 'naith the grun'.'

When the kingie dee'd ae Lammas mirk,
   His fowk made muckle mane,
An' they happit him snod in Walla Kirk
   Wi' this at his cauld head-stane:
'A cheery Craitur's lyin' here'—
   An' they said baith great an' sma',
'He never gar't ane o's shed a tear
   Except when he wore awa'.'

    . . . . .

'Mang heather an' whaups, all' whins an' mist,
   Oh, laughing, lonely hedonist,
   I like to think of you.

The Hermit
(after Béranger)

A HEAP o' fowk like London,
But—losh, nae me!
I couldna' bide i' yon din,
   For ony gowd ye'd gie.
     The clamour o't,
     The glamour o't,
Oh unco sma' they bouk,
   Aside the peace an' quate
O' my ain wee neuk

Oh, fat's a star or chevron?-
   Baubles for a bairn!
Gie me the plash o' Deveron,
   The birr o' rod an' pirn—
     Syne the blythe rest,
     The lythe rest,
Aside a gloamin' stook,
   Wi' the saft stars to benison
My ain wee neuk.

Fat hae I for door-thrashel?
   Twa mile o' yird-fast stane—
At the gell, cheese-press and chassel
   Ringed for a bridle rein—
     A queer beild,
     A drear beild,
But ne'er a lord nor duke
   Craws crouser in his castle

Than me in my wee neuk.

Lane reeks my lum owre corries—
    An'—fa wad foord the linn?
But I rax me doon my Horace,
    An' draw my lug-chair in
        To the peat lowe,
        The sweet lowe,
Anaith the swye an' crook—
    Wi' the aul' collie speldert
Aside me i' the neuk.

A' gane, the fu'-an'-free days,
    Wi' you aul' frien',
A' bye, the you-an-me days,
    Wi' you, bonnie Jean,
        But I've Omar,
        An' I've Homer,
An' turnin' owre my buik,
    I can wile the warld for neipers
I' my ain quate neuk,

Fat mak's the far horizon—
    The bodin', or the bye?
Fat eese oor puir surmisin'
    Owre whither, whence, an' why?
        The fash o't a',
        The clash o't a',
Fa 'll flyte me, gin I jouk
    For the dear Soul's Peace that lies in
My ain wee neuk?

The Cheery Chiel
(after Béranger)

SOUR an' dour wis a' the fowk
    At oor toon-en';
  Mim o' mou', an' lang o' chowk,
    But the hoose an' ben;
  Naething richt, nor oot nor in,
    A'thing aff the reel,
  Till, fustlin' as he tirls the pin,
    In comes the Cheery Chiel.

An' foo we blessed the pow o' him
    Anaith the bauchled tile!
An' cheered the' Hap-an'-Row' o' him
    That gied fae squeak to squile!
At's aul' polonian, losh, we leuch
    Mair than we'd deen sin' Eel.
Ye micht ha heard's abeen the Feugh,
    His an' the Cheery Chiel.

He had a hoosie up the loan,
    A stripie rinnin' by,
A fustle that he tootled on;
    In fee, he'd Earth an' Sky,
An' nae a' plack in pooch or pyok;
    But oh I the couthie beil,
A quinie's face aside the knock
    Made for the Cheery Chiel.

He fiddled, diddled, danced awa',
   Fae parischen to toon;
Newsed i' the neuk wi' aul' gran'da,
   Furled totums wi' the loon.
Laughter and Love—the kingly wares
   He cairriet in his creel—
He niffer't for oor sabs an' sairs,
   The Cheery Chapman Chiel.

Fan nicht cam doon, a' starry, still,
   He prayed his pagan prayer:
'Lord, gie me aye o' Joy my fill;
   Wi' that, I'll seek nae mair;
Aye blythe my fit gaun up the brae,
   An' blythe gaun doon as weel—
At mornin' an' at gloamin' grey,
The same aul' Cheery Chiel.'

. . . . .

Fu', oh fu' 's the weary earth
   O' fowk that greet and girn:
Nae sowl but has its desert dearth,
   Nae back but has its birn—
An' faur's Nepenthe? Nae in a'
   The priest's, the pedant's skeel.
The wit's wi' him that tholes awa',
   An's aye a Cheery Chiel.

MEDITATIONS

The Auld Fisher

I'VE had my pridefu' meenits
  In my lang pilgrimage,
But when a' is said and deen—it's
  Could I turn back Life's page.

I'd tak' ae bonnie mornin'
  Wi' the sun on lea an' hill,
An' the soun' o water churnin'
  Roun' the clapper o' a mill,

An' I'd sit aside my wahnie
  Wi' a deid troot owre my knee—
But ah! '*labuntur anni,*
  Fugaces, Postume.'

The Exile

BURY me not in Egypt!
  Fair is its sun-kissed strand!
But I fain would sleep by some windy steep,
In a far-off northern land.
    For me not the soft hibiscus,
Olive, or palm, or vine;
I'd rest with the heather o'er me
    In that misty land of mine.

Bury me not in Egypt!
    Not by the storied Nile.
On its age-old breast Kings take their rest;
    But away in a cold grey isle
There's a river that's calling, calling,
    There is dust that is kin to me,
And it's there I'd sleep, my children,
    On the braes beside the Dee.

Bury me not in Egypt!
    Towers of the Moslem gleam,
But my dying eyes seek Highland skies,
    And the glint of a moorland stream,
Where the morning winds are blowing,
    And the mists lie chill and low,
And the pibroch pipes me homeward,
    O'er the crags my clansmen know.

Bury me not in Egypt!
    A grave in a Scottish glen

Is beild enough for the last dead Duff,
   So he greets his own again.
And it's not by an alien river,
   'Neath sheen of an orient star,
But in homeland hills you'll lay me
   By my forest Braes o' Mar.

Hame
(St Andrew's Day under the Southern Cross)

GOD bless our land, our Scotland,
  Grey glen an' misty brae,
The blue heights o' the Coolins,
   The green haughs yont the Spey,
The weary wastes on Solway,
   Snell winds blaw owre them a'—
But aye it's Hame, lad,
Yours an' mine, lad,
   Shielin' or ha'.

   It's Hame, it's Hame for ever,
     Let good or ill betide!
   The croon o' some dear river,
     The blink o' ae braeside.

God bless our land; it's yonder—
   Far in the cold North Sea:
But 'neath the old Saint's glamour
   It's calling you and me:
Your feet tread Libyan deserts,
   Mine press the wattle's bloom,
But to-night we stand together
   Among the broom.

   It's Hame, it's Hame for ever,
     Let shore or sea divide!
   The croon o' some dear river,
     The blink o' ae braeside.

God bless our land. We dream o't—
   The days aye brakin' fine
On the lang, lane glints o' heather
   In the glens we kent lang syne.

Ay, we are Reubens, rovers,
   'Neath many an alien star,
But flaunt the blue flag o'er us,
   Pipe up the 'Braes o' Mar,'
And steppe and nullah vanish,
   And pomp and pelf and fame—
It's gloamin'—on a lown hillside,
   An' lads, … We're … Hame.

In Appin

IT'S summer up in Appin;
   An', oh gin it were me,
Owre a hill-road that was steppin',
   Where it's windin' to the sea;
Wi' the whaups a' wheelin' hameward,
An' the muirland spreadin' wide,
   An' ae lad waitin',
   My ain lad waitin'
At the lang dykeside.

It's gloamin' up in Appin,
   An' you an' me oor lanes,
Wi' the burnie's water lappin'
   Owre the green steppin'-stanes;
An' oh the warld was bonnie
When in yours, sae warm and big,
   Ye took my cauld, wee hannie,
   My willin', wee bit hannie
At the aul' shakin' brig.

It's winter up in Appin,
   An' the drift's a' owre Glen Mhor;
But I ken fa 'tis that's chappin',
   Fa's fit comes to the door:
Syne ... ben the hoosie yonder
Was the Land o' Heart's Desire,
   Wi' oor four feet on the fender,
   Yours and mine upon the fender,

Aside oor ain peat-fire.
　Ary we hadna far to wander
　For oor land o' Heart's Desire.

It's owre the years to Appin—
　An', God! fat wad I gie
For ae aul' plaidie happin',
　Oh lad, jist you an' me…
But there's eld upon my broon hair,
An' the red lips ye kissed—
　Life's bye, but for the achin',
　The never-still heart-achin'
For a' that I hae missed.

But we'll baith win back to Appin—
　Some day the sun'll shine
An' the same saft rain be drappin'
　On your grave as on mine.
When there's naithing mair'll pairt us
　Than a strip o kirkyard green—
Ay, Death, lad, will be kinder till's
　Than ever Life has been—
An' it's lythe we'll lie in Appin,
　When the lang day's deen.

A Passport

ONCE long ago I journeyed far,
   'Midst bog, and mire, and wet;
My pilot was one lonely star,
   In a dim horizon set:
And never a fair wind wooed my cheek,
   And never a kindly thing;
But I went—'twas my vagrant pharisee freak—
   To the City of Suffering.

I reached the gate, and souls accurst
   Looked through the bars at me—
'And see,' I cried, 'I come athirst
   For the bliss of ministry.
And kindly words, and good men's gold,
   And women's tears I bring,
The tide of a pitying world has rolled
   To your City of Suffering.'

But through the gloom no warder came
   To open wide to me,
And never a glad voice blessed my name
   For my sweet charity;
But I heard the laugh of an Ishmael,
   Across the grey walls ring:
'Back fool, and learn what it means to dwell
   In our City of Suffering.'

Yet once again I journeyed there,

Back to these souls accurst,
And I said: 'I too have supped with care,
    I too have sorrow nursed;
And a broken heart, and a bleeding brow,
    And my loneliness I bring':
And they cried: 'Come in, you've your passport now,
    To our City of Suffering.'

A Country Sabbath

YONDER the silent hillside,
  Green with the flush of May,
And a lark by the lich-gate singing
  As I murmur, 'Let us pray.'
Dim through the dusky casement
  A vagrant sunbeam creeps,
And I read a chill *Hic jacet*
  Where an old Crusader sleeps.

This is my church. My people.
  God! I have preached at ease,
To cynics who culled their mockings
  From Hegel and Socrates;
To sage and sophist—monarchs
  In the hierarchy of men,
But I stand before you dumbly,
  You toilers of the glen.

Dumb, for my placid dogmas,
  Shibboleths old or new,
Philosophy's poor vagaries—
  What can they be to you?
But the din of some antic tourney
  To warriors worn with fight,
But the echoes of idle revels
  To watchers in the night.

Toil-worn hands and weary,

Furrowed cheek and brow—
Oh, I know the pigmy measure
    Of my nimble nostrums now;
Something for dainty sinnings,
    Something for dainty woes—
But what for the unvoiced sadness
    The joyless toiler knows?

Oh, Culture, shall I curse you?
    Bound in your silken gyves
I have lived till now unknowing
    The pathos of empty lives;
Unknowing and undreaming
    That where the yearlings bleat,
Where the happy wind of summer
    Bends low the bladed wheat.

Where the lint-white's singing pæans,
    There, there are earth's unblest,
The souls that keep unfading
    (Like some sad palimpsest)
Above the ages' imprints,
    One pitying Heart's behest:
'Come, all ye heavy-laden,
    And I will give you rest.'

Come Hame

COME hame, lad, the voice o' the muirland is sayin',
The souch o' the win', an' the water as weel;
'Come hame, lad,' that's aye what the heart o' me's prayin',
At mirk an' at mornin', fae Beltane to Eel.

> Come hame, lad, come hame,
> The Glen's aye the same,
> Lyin' lythe in the land that ye lo'e,
> An' there's weary hearts achin',
> Ay, hearts nigh to breakin',
> For you, lad, for you—for you.

Come hame, lad, fat mak's a' the gowd that ye'll gaither?
    Gin't's muckle ye're winnin', there's mair that ye tine;
An' I ken ye'd gie't a' for your foot on the heather,
    An' your head to the stars, in a glen o' lang syne.
        Come hame, lad, come hame, &c.

Come hame, lad, come hame—or the kent kindly faces
    Will a' be awa' wi' the roch, reivin' years—
An' the tents o' the stranger ye'll find in the places
    Still hallowed by memory's laughter and tears.
        Come hame, lad, come hame, &c.

Come hame, lad, come hame—It's weary wark waitin',
    An' life's slippin' by, an' oor sun's wearin' west:
Tho' yon be the land that ye're grand an' ye're great in,
Come hame ye an' bide in the land ye like best.
        Come hame, lad, come hame, &c.

An Appeal

OH, Glasgow toon is big an' braw,
　　But oh, it's no' for me;
It micht be doon the Broomielaw
　　Gaun soomin' to the sea.

I bite my bannock there the day,
　　An' dee my eident turn,
But aye my heart's on hill an' brae,
　　Aside a norlan' burn.

I stouf aboot the city street,
　　But mid the steer an' din
I'm seein' aye the reekin' peat,
　　The whaups amon' the whin.

Yird-hunger! Aye, it's ill to thole.
　　But fa was't pat it there?
It's ae bit o' the patriot soul
　　The puirest o' 's can share

A whiff o' hame we exiles seek;
　　There's things ye canna gie's—
The gloamin' sun on scaur an' peak,
　　The wash o' island seas—

But let's forgaither here-awa
　　Anaith some kind roof-tree;
To cherish still as brethren a'
　　Dear Land o' Memory.

From the East

UP an' awa, faur the peeweets mourn
    On the blue hill-sides o' hame—
Oh lad, oh lad, gin back we turn,
    Will the glen be aye the same?

Will the broom be growin' on Gauly, lad;
    The slaes by the Ladies' Linn?
Will the aul' bell chime, as it ees't to chime,
    When nicht is creepin' in?

Oh, lad, oh lad, there's a win' that blaws
    Fae yon weary toon to me;
An' I hear the lilt o' convent bells
    Wi' the chaunt o' an Ave Marie,

But I bend my head, an' the stars grow dim
    In the blue of an Eastern sky;
An' I'm stan'in' again where a lintie sings
    An' the Dullan rushes by;

An' I step aince mair owre a rain-washed hill,
    Syne doon a mossy brae
An' it's youth that clarions to me still
    From the Land of Yesterday.

. . . . .

There's a fyackie faul't on a norlan' steep,
    Where a weary heid wad lie;

It's doon an aul' hill road I'd creep
    That's 'naith a norlan' sky,
Wi' winds an' waters soughin' roun'
    A House o' Memory.
Oh, I'd tryst me there wi' a wee bit loon—
    The loon that aince was me.

The End

JIST lift me to the winnock, lass,
    An' lay me canny doon;
I'd like to see the sun again
    Set fair owre field an' toon.
I'm gaun awa' to leave them a',
    On a journey lane an' lang;
But Death has ca'ed fu' kindly,
    An' I'm no' that sweer to gang.

It's jist like fa'in' asleep, lass,
    An' a' my trauchle deen,
To rest my tired bit hannies,
    An' steek my weary een;
To never thole the ruggin' hert,
    The tchave, the fecht, the din,
To never hear the bairnies greet
    For bread I canna win.

It's jist like waukenin' up, lass,
    An' the mornin' brakin' fine
On the lang, lane glints o' heather,
    In a glen I kent lang syne;
Wi' the laverock singin' bonnie
    In a lift that's lown an' blue,
An' father waitin' at the yett,
    Sayin' 'Jeanie, this is you.'

NOTES

The Soldiers' Cairn

This is perhaps the most substantial of the poems published in *Northern Numbers* (T N Foulis: Edinburgh, 1920), pp 125-126.

The Glen's Muster-Roll

J D McClure suggests a contemporary reading of the poem which is worth quoting at length: 'In its references to events in the war (and this poem comes closer than any other I have met to dealing with the war in the terms Hemingway's Frederic Henry lays down—it is densely particular in its use of the actual names of places, units and engagements), the poem emphasises suffering, defeat and death rather than victory. After the confident patriotic swing of the opening lines, the dominie's first personal memory is of Dysie, 'deid an' drooned lang syne' in the torpedoed cruiser Cressy. For the contemporary reader, the ship's name would have immediately called up one of the most traumatic events of the first months of the war, the sinking by a single German submarine, of no less than three armoured cruisers (the others were the Hogue and the Aboukir) off the Dutch coast on 22nd September 1914. Less than 800 men, out of a total complement of 1459 on the three ships, were saved; a sub-head in the *Aberdeen Journal* report on the following day which reads 'Aberdeen man on the Cressy' may account for Mary Symon's use of that particular ship. Dysie's is the first death that comes to mind and perhaps because of that, the dominie is able to invoke the conventional idea of the necessary sacrifice of life to protect the peace and security of home. In the process, the master's picture of the ordinary life of the community is allegorised and the dead man and those like him are turned into emblems, abstracting and distancing what has happened... Thinking about Dysie makes him puzzle about why this landward community has produced so many wanderers; his reference to the three young men, 'exiles on far Australian plains', who have been involved in the Gallipoli fighting, is a reminder that the years just before the war were marked by very heavy out-migration from the North-east, mainly of young men. Gallipoli too was a bitter failure, despite the initial hopes raised by the landings in April 1915, that the operation might shorten the war. The dominie's specific references—to Chanak Bahr (presumably his inaccurate recollection of Chunuk Bair, the rugged massif to the north of Anzac), to Anzac and Lone Pine, are to the scenes of some of the most bitter fighting in an exceptionally bitter campaign and the stanza ends with the winds wailing a requiem over the many dead.' This poem was originally published in the *Aberdeen University Review* and Ian A Olson reprints the piece arranged in long lines of up the 14 words. Ian A Olson (ed.) *No Other Place: poetry from the Aberdeen University Review, 1913-1995* (Tuckwell Press: Edinburgh, 1995), pp 124-125. In the poem, '29' is a reference to the Moray floods of 1829. Sennelager was a German prison camp.

After Neuve Chapelle
The battle of Neuve Chapelle began on 10th March 1915. It was regarded as a British victory although losses exceeded 12,000. 'Street o' Hell' refers to the Rue d'Enfer, a scene of part of the battle.

For Our Empire
A relatively unsuccessful attempt at patriotic verse in English which is not really sufficiently retreived by the switch to Scots and a more elegaic tone in the last line.

The Aucht Day Clock
Published as *The Echt Day Clock* in *Northern Numbers* (T N Foulis: Edinburgh, 1920), pp 123-124.

Wir Roup

Perhaps could be classified as a war poem, but the subject is largely the humours of the locals. This poem was also published as a pamphlet and as such is preserved in the School of Scottish Studies, University of Edinburgh, (F3(4125)). It is dated 30th January, 1918.

The Hedonist

This and the two subsequent poems are translated from the work of Pierre-Jean de Béranger (1780-1857) who was a popular and prolific French songwriter in his time. Walla Kirk refers to a burying-ground on Deveronside.

The Auld Fisher

This poem was printed at the beginning of the first published volume of the poems at the suggestion of William Will. Symon notes in a letter of 30th December 1937: 'it really is an asset as a 'kick-off'.'

The Exile

An explanatory note is appended to the poem in *Deveron Days*: 'The late Duke of Fife died in Egypt, and his body was taken home for interment at Mar Lodge. These lines were suggested by a very fine 'In Memoriam' sermon from the text 'Bury me not in Egypt' preached in the old church of Mortlach by the Reverend J B Cumming.' Printed as a pamphlet, a copy of which is preserved in the Mitchell Libray under the title *The Exile* (821.912).

Hame

Published in *Northern Numbers* (T N Foulis: Edinburgh, 1920), pp 127-128. To celebrate St Andrew's Day in 2015, this poem was projected onto various Scottish landmarks: Kelvingrove Art Gallery, the Usher Hall, the Tron Kirk, Scone Palace, the Glasgow Science Centre and Schiehallion.

From the East

This poem is taken from manuscript: 43. Acc 7534 2. The same version was published in *The Scots Magazine*, Vol 2, No. 4 (January, 1925), p. 241. The last verse only, entitled *The Loon That Aince Was Me*, is published in *Deveron Days*. The reason for this is unclear.

GLOSSARY

Airn—iron.
Aul'—old.
Aumry—cupboard.

Bauchled—misshapen, dented.
Beld—bald.
Ben—parlour end of house.
Bike—wasp or bee hive.
Binnered—dashed noisily.
Birkies—smart young fellows.
Birn—burden.
Bleckies—black people.
Bodin'—looming ahead.
Bouk—bulk.
Bouket—bulked.
Bouk sma'—amount to very little.
Bosie—bosom (also used as a verb).
Bouffin'—bellowing by way of singing.
Bravities—display, adornments.
Breeks—trousers.
Brig—bridge.
Brose—oatmeal dish which was the normal farm breakfast.
Buckie—seashell.
Buckle-beads—a necklace of shells.
Bummies—bees.
Buss—bush.
But an' ben—kitchen and parlour.
Bydand—steadfast (motto of the Gordons).
Bye—past.
By-ordinar—unusual.

Canny—gentle.
Carritches—catechism.
Chancy—uncertain.
Chapman—an itinerant merchant.
Chap—strike (as a clock). Knock (at the door).

Chappet—wealed and discoloured by cold.

Chaumer—men's sleeping-place at a farm.

Chumley-cheek—fireside.

Cheep—a feeble sound.

Cheeper—a contemptuous way of referring to a modern mantelpiece clock, with its (relatively) weak chime.

Cheese-press and chassel—a stone erection with an inside tub for making cheese.

Chippet in—interpolated.

Chouk:—cheek.

Clapper—mill contrivance which shakes the hopper.

Clash-—noisy disagreement or chatter.

Cleeter-clatter—a recurring rattling noise.

Clort—mess.

Clour—hurt.

Clyte—a fall or the noise there-from.

Crap o' the wa'—in a stone and lime building the space between the top of the wall and the roof: a common depot for odds and ends.

Craw—boast.

Creel—basket.

Crouse—proud.

Crook—the iron hook and chain suspended from 'the swye', where the pots and kettles are hung over a peat fire.

Croon—low-sung song.

Cushey-doo—cushat-dove, woodpigeon.

Dambrod—draughtboard.

Dhubrack—sea trout when it comes up an inland river.

Dicht—wipe.

Doch-an-doris—parting glass.

Doiterin'—walking slowly and erratically.

Doo's neck silk—so called because of a changing iridescence like that on the neck of a pigeon.

Doss—bunch.

Dother—daughter.

Dreetlin'—dropping.

Dub—mud.

Ducksh'ner—dictionary.
Dud—dress, clothing.
Dwawm—a feeling of enervation; on the borderland of a swoon, but not quite so definitely away with it.

Eel—Yule.
Ees't—used.
Ern (Arn)—the alder.
Ettled—intended.

Fa—who.
Fa'—fall.
Fash—trouble.
Faul't—folded.
Flype—turn inside out.
Flyte—scold, reprove.
Foo—how.
Foun'—foundation.
Fowin' peats—cutting the turf and letting up to dry.
Fowk—folk.
Fozel—wheeze.
Fremmit—strange, foreign.
Fuged—played truant.
Fulp—whelp, puppy.
Fustlin'—whistling.
Futtled—whittled.
Fykes o' phrase—niceties of diction.
Fyackie—plaid.

Gairten—garter.
Geat—child.
Gell—gable of a house.
Geylies—rather.
Gied—went.
Gi'e's 't—give it to us.
Gowket—stupid.
Grauvit—knitted wool neck-scarf.
Greet—weep.

Groff—thick, large.
Groff-write—the large text handwriting done by young scholars.

Habber—stammer.
Halflin—a between-man-and-boy farm-hand.
Hauf-fou—half-drunk.
Hairst-bap—a specially big, flat, round roll used for the harvest-field 'piece'.
Haiver-talk—pointless talk.
Hannie—diminutive of han', hand.
Hanky—pocket handkerchief.
Hansel—reward.
Hantle—much.
Hap—to cover.
Hicks and mants—stammers and stutters.
Hirples—limps.
Houst or hoast—cough.
Horn-en'—the parlour or best end (where the horn spoons were used as against the iron ones of the kitchen).
Howe—hollow.

Ill-faured—ugly.

Jaud—a Jade; applied to a woman or girl, it may mean anything from gentle jocularity to severe condemnation.
Jow—the soft sound made by an oscillation of any kind.
Jouk—evade, avoid (say, by bending as from a missile).

Kink-hoast—whooping-cough.
Kist o' drawers—chest of drawers.
Kitlins—kittens.
Knock—clock.
Kyaak—cake.

Laich—low.
Laich—chanted softly, sung.
Leuch—laughed.
Lichtlied—jilted, deceived, made light of.

Loan—roadway between fields.
Loon—boy.
Losh!—mild swear word. a euphemism for 'Lord'.
Loupet—leaped.
Lown—quiet.
Lug—ear.
Lum—chimney.
Lum—silk hat.
Lythe—sheltered.

Mane—moan, mourning.
Meen—moon.
Men't—mended.
Mim o' mou—silent.
Mislippen—distrust, question.
Moufu'—mouthful.
Muntin's—mountings, adornments.
Mous—nearly always used along with the negative 'nae mous': not
to be sneered at; striking, important.
Muckle—much.
Mullie—snuff-mull, box kept in the pocket for holding snuff.
Murlacks—crumbs.
Mutch—woman's cap.
Myaukens—hares.

'Naith—beneath.
Neiper—neighbour.
Neeps—turnips.
Neist—next.
Neuk—nook.
Newfangled—novel; generally used with a suggestion of contempt
or derision.
Newsed—chatted.
Nib—nose.
Nicht-kep—night-cap.
Niffert—exchanged.
Nowt—cattle.

Oolet—owl.
Ooled—overawed, cowed.
Owre-croon mutch—a woman's dress cap, which stood out high above the head.

Pandrop—a hard round sweetie.
Paumer-saunter—wander about aimlessly.
Pech—pant.
Peeweet—lapwing.
Pim—reel of a fishing-rod.
Pouk—poke.
Pow—head.
Powet—tadpole.
Pree—taste.
Puddock—frog; applied to a person in various ways, from the frankly contemptuous to the amicably jocular.
Pumphel—square church pew.

Quaich—a two-eared drinking cup.
Queet—ankle.
Quine, quinie—girl.

Rax—reach, stretch.
Reek—smoke.
Reekin' lum—smoking chimney.
Red-up—make tidy.
Red-wud—raging mad.
Reivin'—despoiling, ravaging.
Roch—rough, uncouth.
Roset—resin.
Rude—inelegant.
Ryve nor rug—neither split nor break in any way.

Sanshach—self-complacent.
Sark—shirt.
Sauch—the willow.
Saut—salt.
Sclaffer—shuffle noisily with the feet.

Sconeface—face like a scone or girdle-cake, round, flat, highly coloured.

Shalt—pony.

Sheemach—matted.

Shielin'—hillside or moorland cottage.

Shoggly—shaky.

Sib till's a'—akin to us all.

Skailies—slate-pencils.

Skeel—skill.

Skirl—scream, yell.

Sklates—school slates.

Skyte—a mouthful (of spirits).

Sloke—slake, quench thirst.

Sma' —small.

Smiddy—smithy.

Sneeshan—snuff.

Snell—keen cold.

Snod—neat, snug.

Soochin' —sighing murmurously.

Sook—suck.

Sowf—breathe heavily.

Speldert—lying flat, at full stretch.

Speel—climb.

Spiert—enquired.

Squile—squeal.

Starnies—stars.

Stilpert—long, lanky (like stilts).

Stook—eight sheaves of corn or barley set up two and two against each other on the harvest field to dry.

Stoupet-bed—a bed supported by posts.

Stripe, stripie—a rill, streamlet.

Sumph—a lout.

Swack—smart.

Sweer—lazy.

Swye—the pivoted iron bar from which the crook hangs above the peat fire.

Tappit-hen—a vessel for holding liquor.

Teem—empty.
Thole—bear, endure.
Thrashel—threshold.
Threeps—protestations.
Tile—dress hat.
Tirl-at-the-pin—to rattle at the door asking for admittance.
Tow—string.
Tosselled—tasselled.
Tootle—play on a wind instrument.
Trok—anything trumpery.
Troot—trout.
Trackies—tracts.
Tummel—tumble.
Tyke—dog.
Tyaavin'—struggling.

Unco—uncommon, uncommonly, with a secondary meaning, as in 'unco folk'—strangers.

Wag-at-the-wa' —a hanging clock with the weights and chains uncovered, and the pendulum oscillating ('wagging') at the wall.
Wahnie—wand (diminutive), fishing rod.
Wanworth—worthless person.
Weesht—hush.
Weskit—waistcoat.
Weyvin'—weaving.
Whaup—curlew.
Winnock—window.
Wir—our.
Wirsel's—ourselves.

Yapp—hunger, craving.
Yammer—a monotonous persistent cry.
Yeanling—a newly born lamb.
Yird-fast—firmly fixed in the ground.

HOG'S BACK

These poems are set in Bembo,
a typeface cut by Francesco
Griffo in 1495 for the works of
Pietro Bembo, a poet, a Cardinal
and lover of Lucrezia Borgia.